Labyrinth

Beth Steel's first play *Ditch* premiered at the HighTide Festival before transferring to the Old Vic Tunnels. *Ditch* was shortlisted for the John Whiting Award. Her second play, *Wonderland*, was a finalist for the Susan Smith Blackburn Prize and won her the Charles Wintour Award for Most Promising Playwright at the Evening Standard Theatre Awards 2014.

BETH STEEL

Labyrinth

FABER & FABER

First published in 2016
by Faber and Faber Limited
74–77 Great Russell Street,
London WC1B 3DA

Typeset by Country Setting, Kingsdown, Kent CT14 8ES
Printed and bound by CPI Group (UK) Ltd, Croydon CR0 4YY

A CIP record for this book
is available from the British Library

ISBN 978-0-571-33343-1

For Rowan

Acknowledgements

This is a play about debt and I have accrued many while researching and writing it. I would like to thank:

Everyone at the Hampstead Theatre, profoundly, for staging my work so spectacularly and for the all the hard work and love that goes into that. Andrew Edwards, Richard Howell and Max Pappenheim for their mighty creative brains. All the very brilliant actors and John Ross for bringing the labyrinth to life. Tariq Ali, Sebastian Budgen, Adam Curtis for research suggestions. The Peggy Ramsay Foundation for a grant. Yaddo and the MacDowell Colony for solitude. Isabella and Luciano Biancardi for Nice. Pawel Wojtasik for New York. Caitlin McLeod, Adam Penford, DinahWood and Steve King for their encouragement. Sebastian Born for his committed championing. Jennie Miller for being the most wonderful agent. Lin and Ken Craig for their generosity. My mum, my dad, Amy and Will for their love and support.

Greg Ripley-Duggan, producer and pillar, for his utter passion and faith; for getting us here.

The marvellous Anna Ledwich for being nothing short of a revelation. This play would not be what it is without her gifts.

Rowan, for enduring all the elation, doubt, and tears; for willing this play into being. I would not be the writer I am without you.

Introduction

When you first encounter something, it's not often apparent that it will change your life.

There are the small things: I was living on a Greek island when a tourist left a glossy magazine behind and inside was an article about the playwright Sarah Kane. I eventually lost the magazine but not the article. A year later I was living in London and waitressing. With my first week's wages I bought Sarah Kane's collected plays.

And there are the big things: when Lehman Brothers collapsed and the world banking system looked set to follow, I was, for the first time in my life, gripped by a political event. The world outside my own head had never been as vivid, as interesting to me, until that point. (This was not merely an over-extended adolescence or temperament; there were just gaps in my thinking the size of canyons.) But this event fascinated me – it was vast, almost cosmic. All these moving pieces impacting and changing each other.

I recently discovered that the word history comes from the Ancient Greek *istoria* and means 'inquiry'. Such a word has roots so deep that, even after the word itself has been cut away, its meaning continues to grow, and I still feel its phantom branches. At some point I stopped reading about our present financial turmoil and inquired about Marx, Keynes and Freidman; about the New Deal, Gold Standard and Glass Steagall; about Pinochet, Thatcher and Reagan . . .

History is a huge landscape to dig into and writing this play has been something of an excavation. I spent a long time wondering just what it is I'm digging out. My first instincts are always wrong when determining what a play might be. I spent six months researching the military Junta in Argentina *and* behavioural economics, believing I was writing a play about torture and finance.

When I finally came upon the Latin American debt crisis, the parallels with today weren't immediately apparent. It took time to digest the event and everything that preceded and followed. But when I said to Edward Hall, with some excitement and incoherence, that I was going to write about a debt crisis that had happened thirty years ago on the other side of the world, his reaction was: 'I have no idea what you're talking about – go for it.' A wonderful leap of faith and exactly what I needed.

Being inside the research was something I loved – although depending on the day, also abhorred. The daily mental activity of it; the piecing together of the puzzle. But the most confounding part of writing this play was not the research itself but how to bring it to life. How to imaginatively embody the facts, figures and thinking. The clues for which often came to me as images. An example of this was when, months into my titleless and still somewhat directionless play, I saw a lone desk in the middle of the stage, red corridors of light on the floor mapping out a labyrinth, the desk at its centre. Seated behind the desk was a man wearing formal trousers and nothing else – I knew he was a banker. The light began to dim, and as it did, the bare-chested banker mounted the desk and ate a globe. This image does not appear in the play; the visual fragments I think of as offerings, portals that take me closer to what I'm trying to say, as I ask myself: Why did I see that? What exactly does it mean? I wasn't entirely sure at that stage, but I had my title.

Writing a play is, for me, a sculptural thing; a summoning of shapes and textures through voices. Hearing them emerge is a really exciting thing. There were characters that walked out of my mind immediately, characters I caught glimpses of and doggedly ran after, characters who only made their entrance long after everyone else had showed up. This was true of Frank – and his appearance changed the fabric of the play.

The warping fabric of this play was a surprise: euphoric and often debilitating. I have previously written out of sequence, at least in the beginning of a play. This was different. It came in order, but a mental block immediately followed the concluding of each of the acts; I had no idea how I was going to continue it. The play turned into an ice sheet, impenetrable; I was left staring at its surface. Eventually something would give way, a way through would appear. In such moments it felt like the play was ahead of me, as if it knew exactly where it was going, and I had to trust its direction. Of course this is less hocus-pocus than it sounds: it's relentless conscious graft that opens the door. Nevertheless, there was a feeling the play was working me, not the other way around.

As a writer who believes a play isn't mine, this makes perfect sense. Once I'd finished *Labyrinth*, this feeling intensified. It was as if it had always been there, existing in the dark without me. I am sure this is in part due to the fact that I'm writing from lived events and drawing on the work of many writers, journalists and economists.

In the first week of rehearsal it was an economist, Dr Ingrid Bleynat, who came into rehearsal along with Dr. Paul Segal to talk about the events of the play with myself, Anna Ledwich and the cast. Among the many interesting things she said was this: economists don't learn history. They are taught mathematics and models, but not history.

It was Herodotus, the Ancient Greek historian, who said history is one of the strangest things we humans do, all this asking and searching. To me, however, the opposite is true. In the Greek myth of Theseus and the Minotaur, Theseus made his way out of the labyrinth having been given a ball of thread by Ariadne, allowing him to retrace his path. How are we to find our way out of the labyrinth if we are not given a thread?

Beth Steel
August 2016

Labyrinth was first performed at Hampstead Theatre, London, on 1 September 2016. The cast was as follows:

John Sean Delaney
Charlie Tom Weston Jones
Rick Eric Kofi Abrefa
Frank Philip Bird
Howard Martin McDougall
L.B. Holmes Alexia Traverse-Healy
Philip Matt Whitchurch
Grace Elena Saurel

Other parts played by the ensemble:
 Joseph Balderrama, Ryan Ellsworth,
 Abubakar Salim, Christopher Sawalha

Director Anna Ledwich
Assistant Director Celine Lowenthal
Designer Andrew D. Edwards
Production Manager Alison Ritchie
Lighting Designer Richard Howell
Sound Designer Max Pappenheim
Movement Director John Ross
Dialect Coach Penny Dyer
Costume Supervisor Sabrina Cuniberto
Casting Directors Crowley Poole

Characters

John

Howard

Charlie

Rick

Philip

Frank

Grace

L.B. Holmes

Banker

Brazilian Minister

American Businessman

Hostess

Trent

Bartender

Security Guard 1

Security Guard 2

Mexican Minister

Figure

Penguin

Argentinian Minister

Character 1

Character 2

Treasury

Banker 1

Banker 2

IMF/Fund

Beggar

Pensioner

Mexican Spectre

The cast play multiple roles

LABYRINTH

When we thought we were at the end,
we came out again at the beginning.

Plato

Act One

ONE

New York. The Bank. 1978.
  Howard Richman's office.
  Howard, fifties, lets loose a red yo-yo or holds it in his hand like an apple.
  John Anderson, early twenties, is wearing a thick wool suit on a hot summer's day.

Howard You know what business we're in?

John Yes, sir. Banking.

Howard Optimism. That's the business we're in. Take a seat.

John Thank you, sir.

Howard Unbutton your jacket.

John Thank you, sir.

Howard And tell me why I should hire you.

  Little pause.

John Well . . .

Howard I got guys here from Harvard. Princeton. Bright guys. Degrees, Masters, you name it, they got it. Where'd you go to college, John?

John (*clears throat*) It wasn't Harvard, sir.

Howard Just as I thought.

John Mr Richman, I –

Howard Walter Richman, my great-grandfather, was loading the Union cannon at the age of thirteen. Three

3

years later, the Civil War over, he strikes out on his own in Dakota. Now people believe that the pioneers headed into the Plains, lived tough, bred hard and founded themselves ranch dynasties. The reality: those Plains were like a Bermuda Triangle, many people just disappeared. But not my great-grandfather. With the help of three wives – the first wife died in childbirth, I'm not sure what happened to the other one – he had a dirty brood of kids and raised himself a herd of cattle. Walter Richman *died* in his saddle.

Henry Richman, my grandfather, watched the last of that cattle give in to a terrible winter before buying a one-way ticket west saying, 'Well, it can't get no worse than this.' Working down a Utah coal mine convinces him otherwise. Several explosions later and homesick for a saddle, he signs up for the Spanish–American War, saying, 'Well, it can't be no worse than this.' He takes a bullet in the neck, survives, and gets into the life insurance business, where he prospered saying, 'Well, it can't get better.' And it didn't: Henry Richman *died* faking his own death.

George Richman, my father, is sixteen – having lied to the recruiting officer – when he steps into the bloody trenches of Europe's Western Front. Not one, but two prisoner-of-war camps later, he's bringing the Sunbeam iron into the hearts and homes of America. A managerial position at General Electric follows before getting into real estate and local politics. George Richman *died* on a golf course.

John Those are very inspiring stories, sir.

Howard Inspiration got nothing to do with it and nor did Harvard. What do you know about Latin America?

John Latin America?

Howard You speak Spanish?

John *Un poco.*

Howard stares expressionless.

No, sir, I don't. But I've always loved Spanish.

Howard The Latin American division may have an opening for a loan officer . . .

John I can be fluent inside of six months.

Howard idly flicks through a report.

It's true I didn't go to Harvard, sir. Instead, I put myself through grad school at night working two jobs. Nobody wants this opportunity more than me. Nobody works harder than me, nobody *can* work harder than me: I don't need sleep. I don't do lunchbreaks. I am an animal. I am insane.

Finally Howard looks up.

Howard Cookie?

John takes what he's offered.

Well, look at that. They've had the sense to use cinnamon. My wife's cookies always have cinnamon.

John My father said he married my mother for her cookies.

Howard I married Margie for the sex. (*Looks at the file.*) You've been a credit analyst for . . . ?

John A year.

Howard Ten months. (*Closes the file.*) The job track can be blisteringly fast. I'm going to put you under Charlie Hewitt's wing, my star loan officer for Latin America.

John I . . . I'd be honoured, sir.

Howard See that smoke over there? In the old days you put a bank where there was smoke. Like old Rockefeller said, 'Where there's smoke, there's money.' That's how it was for most of this century. Now, and in less than a decade, we're chasing smoke in seventy countries on every continent of this planet.

John The expansion's been truly incredible.

Howard We didn't go overseas, son, because we *wanted* to. We went because we *had* to. Twenty per cent of American goods and services are now sold overseas. One out of every five American jobs is created by those foreign sales. The corporations, our clients, want us – damn well expect us – to finance their international trade . . . be it on the edges of the civilised world. Course, every country was once a developing country. To the English bankers of the nineteenth century, America was a country mired in default. Somewhere down the line we've all relied on foreign money . . .

I suggest you start familiarising yourself with the continent.

John Yes, sir, I'll start looking at the WB, IDA, IM . . .

Howard has resumed working.

Thank you, sir.

John makes to leave.

Howard John . . . one more thing. In my experience, a man fond of acronyms is a man set on reducing the world in order to try and make sense out of it. Better to know from now that it's too big, messy and complicated for that.

TWO

The Bank.
   A series of clocks showing local time in Tehran, London, Geneva, New York . . .

6

Bankers on the phone – dialling, redialling, switching languages, and this is constant. In the foreground and on the move:

Charlie Your *job*, what do you say your name was?

John John Anderson.

Charlie *John Anderson* is to be my underling because knowing a liability from an asset *doesn't* make you a loan officer.

John But Mr Richman –

Charlie Put you with me to determine your future and right now, just looking at you, I doubt you have one. (*Stops.*) *Where* did you get that suit?

John I, um . . . I don't know.

Charlie Neither do I. That's your first mistake. One look and I should be able to price you by the yard, unspool you all the way back to the bolt at Brooks Brothers. Before you can think like a loan officer you've got to look like one. And you're going to have to adjust to the pace. Which division were you in before?

John Asia Pacific.

Charlie Total static lending zone. Latin America, hyperkinetic. These last ten days I've been to Brazil, Peru, Paraguay. Over there I'm calling on six or seven clients a day, every day, selling them loans. So if you think the life of a loan officer is lounging on a beach in Rio de Janeiro with a *fantastic* piece of ass, think again, you're on a red-eye over the Andes looking for more loan opportunities in one of the fastest growing areas of the world . . .
    You've been? Latin America.

John No.

Charlie The ass is fantastic but they're all fucking crazy.

Rick and Philip, sitting side by side, cradling phones between ear and shoulder.

Rick The last one stabbed him with a fork.

Charlie I was leaving, she was upset.

Philip The one before that burnt his passport.

Charlie Sometimes I miss the Philippines. You get none of that in the Philippines.

Rick In the Philippines you walk out of the airport and there's a girl free with the car.

Philip Always a Jaguar in the Philippines. Bangkok . . .

Rick Silver Lincoln.

Philip Hong Kong.

Rick Rolls-Royce.

Philip Saudi Arabia.

Rick Stretch Mercedes.

Philip Indonesia.

Rick Porsche.

Charlie Between the three of us our portfolios surpass the reach of the Ottoman Empire. That's Robert Fisher's office, Vice President of our division. I know what you're thinking but actually he's thirty-two and frankly, if you *haven't* made Vice President by thirty-two you're a loser. How old are you, Rick?

Rick (*now on the phone, mouths*) Fuck you.

Charlie Four years ago, everything you see before you did not exist. We are the pioneers of global finance – and we write the rules. The grey-haired crowd of decades past are gone, Wall Street is ours. We took it. And we're just getting started . . .

If you do stick around, the Latin American division is *the* place to be. For sheer loan volume size, nowhere else in the third world comes close. Brazil, Mexico, Venezuela: among the top ten borrowing countries *in the world*.

He arrives at John's desk.

I want you to write a risk report for an Argentinian loan I have on the go.

John But Mr Richman said . . . I think maybe there's been a misunderstanding. You see, I was a credit analyst but . . .

Charlie There's assholes on every floor of this building. You don't get to be an asshole unless you're making money – serious money. Until then you're nothing. So get reading. Oh . . . and have a nice day.

John looks more closely at the pile on his desk as Charlie walks off.

John But . . . they're in Spanish?

Charlie So?

John I don't speak Spanish.

Charlie Get a dictionary.

THREE

The Bank.
  Rick and Philip, their feet up, reading Euromoney *and the* Wall Street Journal.

Rick I met Caroline for dinner.

Philip You're back there?

Rick I had dinner, she had cantaloupe.

Philip What is it with her and melon?

Rick Total erasure: her goal.

Philip I went for a drink with Patrick. No dinner.

Rick The gangster?

Philip Patrick?

Rick Every time he asks a question he puts on a gangster voice.

Philip He just got back from Seoul. He ate *live* octopus. *Whole.*

Rick (*demonstrates voice*) Whole?

Philip Whole.

Rick (*demonstrates again*) How big an octopus are we talking?

Philip Including eight squirming arms and a bulbous head, size of your palm. Imagine getting all of that in your *mouth*. He said three arms stuck to his cheek for a while, and that once in, despite committed chewing, the suction cups were still *active*. All part of the delicacy, apparently, the sensation of it climbing back up your throat. *Never* let a Korean order for you.

Rick Did he make the loan?

Charlie appears at John's desk.

Charlie How would you like a week in the Caribbean?

John The Caribbean?

Charlie Our Grand Cayman office needs some attention. Well?

John I . . . I'd love to go.

Charlie Great.

John (*startled*) Alright.

Charlie Follow me.

John beams, even adopts a swagger similar to Charlie's. They stop in front of a solitary desk, Charlie puts on a pair of sunglasses.

Welcome to the Caribbean.

Rick and Philip snort and howl with laughter. John is mortified.

What? You don't think this is an island?

John It's a desk.

Charlie Well I say this desk is in the Caribbean and the Fed and the IRS say the same.
As far as the authorities are concerned this desk is in the Atlantic. It's offshore. Therefore everything we do from this desk is done offshore.

Little pause.

John There's no Cayman office?

Charlie There's a brass plate. And a lawyer. Enough for tax-free status.

John Is that . . . legal?

Laughter from Philip and Rick.

Charlie It's a fiscal invention. You believe it, they believe it.

A staffer dumps a ton of paperwork on John's new desk.

Charlie And make sure you use the Cayman branch logo, I designed it myself.

Staffer instructs John as Charlie heads back to his chair. A Banker appears.

Banker You've been to Saudi Arabia, right? I'm going out next week.

Charlie Congratulations.

Banker Thanks. So, like, anything I ought to know?

Philip Homosexual activity carries the death penalty.

Banker Fuck you.

Charlie Do not encourage Western air hostesses to go topless around the pool.

Rick You know there's no liquor, right?

Banker Course I know –

Charlie Don't show the sole of your foot.

Banker What?

Philip 'Yes' means 'possibly'.

Charlie Eat only with your right hand.

Rick Don't gesture with your left.

Philip *Never* enquire after the wellbeing of your host's wife.

Charlie And be careful in taxis.

Banker What's wrong with taxis?

Charlie If they crash you are personally responsible and therefore *liable* for all damages, injuries, and loss of life.

Banker But I'm just the passenger?

Charlie But the driver would not have had the accident had you not hired him to take your Western ass back to your air-conditioned room at the Intercontinental.

Banker But that's fucked.

Charlie That's the Koran.

Banker What do I do?

Howard Charlie!

Charlie leaves them to it and heads for Howard's office.

Rick So what's the tour?

Banker Jeddah, Riyadh, Kuwait, Tehran, Damascus . . .

Rick You doing Israel?

Philip Charlie did heaps of business in Israel.

Rick He's even got a kibbutz named after him.

Philip A forest, Rick. He's got a forest.

Rick Same thing. They fucking love him.

Philip Get your passport cleansed in Cyprus first.

Charlie stands before John's desk.

Charlie You're coming with me on a trip.

John Where now? The Bahamas?

Charlie Brazil.

John lifts his head up.

We're going to Brazil.

FOUR

Rio de Janeiro. Beach. Evening.
John and Charlie, stockinged feet, bottle of champagne each.

Charlie My mother's an all-American bitch. My father, an anachronism from the fifties. A self-sacrificing, loyal company man who's over-identification with that company has arrested his mobility. Needless to say, I don't share my father's values. Not that the world that belonged to him exists any more anyway. Our generation woke up and smelt the coffee: sorry, folks, we no longer provide a deal for everybody. You don't get to have a cushy corporate job for life by being well-liked and having a socially gifted wife. As for being an autoworker and owning your own home whilst putting two kids through college? Don't make me laugh. That America went out the window with rising energy costs.

John Would you have wanted it? A cushy corporate job for life.

Charlie The sentence alone makes me think of prostate cancer. I have no nostalgia for *that* America.

John The cars were pretty good.

Charlie When a European says to you, 'That's history,' they have blood vessels popping out of their neck, such is their reverence for the past. When we say it, we're saying something's over . . .

John That's history.

Charlie Done with.

John Move on.

Charlie The past is not only irrelevant, it's dangerous. Not enough people know this . . .
    What about your father?

John My father . . .?

Charlie What does he do?

John Oh . . . he's dead.

Charlie Shit.

John Yeah. I had to make my own way.

Charlie is staring at John.

Charlie Don't you wear glasses?

John No.

Charlie I'd swear you wore glasses. Are you sure?

John Yes.

Charlie Really?

John Definitely.

Charlie You should.

John Wear glasses?

Charlie You look like a guy who wears glasses. It's confusing if you don't.

John Why'd you go into banking?

Charlie I'd be an idiot not to. Banking is exploding and credit's the hub. Money is like water, it's looking for a place to go. The Middle East is *awash* with petrodollars from the oil crisis, petrodollars they deposit with us – there only being so many Palm Spring condos and Swiss chalets they can buy – and we lend it to the third world to pay its energy bills.

John Everybody's a winner.

Charlie Neither a borrower nor a lender be. Shakespeare. What the fuck did he know? (I used to be quite literary in college.)

Trust me, fifteen years from now, having flown – with two passports from the State Department – first class around the world and having slept with its most beautiful women, I will retire a rich man. White-pillared house, an attractive wife, two smart kids; a place out in the Vineyard or Cape, and a fuck-pad in the city. I will sit on the board of various companies and play a *lot* of golf.

John I want to make a pile of money. Be respected . . .

Charlie Respected? You don't want to be respected. You want to be *envied*.

John Do you really have two passports from the State Department?

Charlie Yes, I do.

John This is the furthest I've been from home.

Charlie Feels good, doesn't it?

John Feels . . . *great*.

Charlie You get used to it after a while. Like most things.
  Death waits in the first world. There's exceptions. But on the whole it waits. Gets in line. There's an order to it. You're born. Your children are born. Your children's children are born. You die. Your children die. Your children's children die. In the third world . . . there's no order to death. First time here, you realise that. You realise . . . and then you forget . . .
  I forget which country I'm in half the time. On a thousand dollars a day everywhere's a lot like New York.

John I appreciate it, Charlie, being here. Most of my life I've been running to catch a bus everyone else I knew had a reserved seat on.

Charlie You take the *bus*?

John No. No, I . . . Doesn't matter.
  Is it true Mr Richman takes the stairs?

Charlie What?

John Every morning, twenty-four floors?

Charlie Is it true?

John Yeah.

Charlie You're asking me?

Charlie laughs.

John What's so funny?

Charlie Even the ocean sounds false to me. Even the ocean.

He makes to leave.

John Where are you going?

Charlie Get another bottle. Two bottles. And cigars. You smoke cigars? Sure you do.

He turns back to John.

And John . . . don't try so hard.

FIVE

Brazil. The Minister's home.
  Two men appear with Charlie, smoking cigars: a Brazilian Minister, wearing military uniform, and an American businessman.
  A bodyguard holds an AK47.

Charlie (*whispers*) Be nice, he shoots people.

John looks away from the guard and to a cross on a wall.

Minister When my countrymen look at the cross, we are looking at Christ's suffering. You Americans are not interested in that. Americans are all about the empty cross. The rising. This is what you worship. *Rising.* Brazil can learn from that.

Charlie You've made substantial gains these last years.

Minister Before the oil crisis we were growing at eleven per cent.

American When I hear people call Brazil a developing country, I say to them: a GNP the tenth largest in the world. *That's* developing?

Minister We have our problems but we are a country of continental size with worldwide ambitions.

Charlie My bank wants you to realise that potential.

Minister Brazil's growth is in everybody's interest. As President Kennedy once said, a rising tide lifts all boats . . .
   Please, sit.
   In my grandfather's house there was a map of the world on the wall, upside down. People would say to him. 'Your map is wrong. The South is in the North.' He never changed it. A mischievous man, my grandfather.

Charlie I often hear people say Brazil looks like America did to the English a hundred years ago. It could collapse. Or it could become one of the great world powers.

Minister But not without energy. Energy is what we need: more energy, more growth. Right now, my government has more than one hundred state projects in energy and transport under construction. Construction's *the* most profitable industry here . . . after banking, of course. Brazil is not a country any more, it's a market.

   Laughter.

A construction site from north to south.

American You name it, my company's building it.

Minister But this power plant is the most important project of them all.

   Minister produces files all round.

Minister And the most expensive.

Charlie My bank's used to dealing with loans of this size and more. Martin's been a client of ours for a number of years now, we've financed his trade here –

American Across all of Latin America.

Charlie We made our first loan here four years ago and we've been here ever since. I know a lot of banks who *want* to invest in Brazil but their judgement is that it's a land of tomorrow – and tomorrow is not here. My view? That day is here. We look beyond the problems and see the possibilities.

Minister This power plant will transform the lives of our very poorest people: access to energy for all! The costs are outlined in here: clearing of the rainforest, resettlement, construction . . . We have quotes from three construction companies, Martin's included. My government is yet to decide to whom we will award the contract.

Charlie Of course.

Charlie and John look briefly at their files.

Minister Only a decade ago, we would approach banks for the very smallest of loans and they would have nothing to do with it. Reminds me of a joke I heard: a banker's someone who gives you money when you *don't* need it.

*

The Minister and American Businessman are engaged in conversation.
Charlie and John are aside, John referring to the file.

John Martin's bid for the construction contract is thirty per cent higher.

Charlie So?

John So they're not going to award him the contract.

Charlie Because his bid's thirty per cent higher? It's practically a done deal.

John But that's . . .?

Charlie Connections. That's *connections*. And what Latin America's all about.

John But that's . . .

Charlie's expression: 'What?'

A waste . . . of government money.

Charlie That's not our concern.

John No, sure, but . . .

Charlie Our concern is securing the loan. Period.

John Right. I'm just trying to understand why they're prepared to pay more?

Charlie I already told you why.

John Because they're friends?

Charlie Because business is never a one-way street.

He checks back at the Minister and Businessman.

John He's paid?

Charlie You mean bribed? That would be unlawful.

John Then what?

Charlie Politicians aren't in politics for ever. He may one day sit on the board of a certain construction company. He may even wind up a director of our bank . . .

Remember your first beer? How awful it was? Sometimes the good things taste bad at first.

Charlie joins the Minister and Businessman; drinks are poured; glasses raised.

SIX

Brazil. Golf course. Afternoon.

Charlie is practising, his caddie offering him different clubs.

John, not dressed for the game, a little breathless and sweating, appears.

John Charlie . . . I've been looking everywhere for you.

Charlie I said we'd meet after lunch.

John I need to talk to you.

Charlie I'm a little busy here.

John It's about the loan. I've been –

Charlie (*to the caddie*) Bring me a water. And make it cold.

The caddie leaves.

Babaca. Never talk business.

John Sorry. *Babaca?*

Charlie It's Portuguese for asshole.

John I didn't know you spoke Portuguese?

Charlie I make an effort to learn terms of abuse in all languages. What is it?

John I've been doing a little digging.

Charlie Digging?

John Some research. Every power plant that's ever been built here has overrun on costs. Some of these power plants aren't even operational.

Charlie When'd you find the time to do this?

John What? Oh, in my room, I –

Charlie You'd look better with a tan. You know that? You should really hit the pool.

John Sure, okay, but . . . so, so these power plants aren't operational. Five, seven, eight years later, hundreds of *millions* over budget, and *not even* operational. And here's the kicker: Martin's company has never constructed a power plant before, which makes it's even more likely to overrun on costs!

  Little pause.

Charlie That's it?

John You don't . . . think that's a problem?

Charlie Nope.

John Right. I mean, I know you want Martin to have the contract –

Charlie Martin, Martin, I don't give a fuck about Martin. I *do* give a fuck about the loan.

John Exactly: this plant will be a black hole that swallows money. This loan is –

Charlie Government guaranteed, asshole. That's what it is. And all I care about.

John You don't care if it overruns by hundreds of millions?

Charlie It overruns, it overruns.

John Or worse, never becomes operational?

Charlie What do you care?

John Because a loan has to fund an investment that goes on to *create* a cash flow.

Charlie We won't be left holding the bag.

John That's how a loan is repaid. Isn't that textbook lending?

Charlie Textbook? You're in the real world now. This is a country the size of a continent, not a factory in Cleveland. Countries don't go bankrupt. Their infrastructure doesn't go away, their natural resources don't go away. Their assets always exceed their liabilities. The *only* thing left to do now is write a rosy risk report for Howard and the committee that will push it through. Keep it brief and bland. The blander the better.

Charlie gets back to his golf.

John You want me to write it?

Charlie Consider it an opportunity.

John Why can't you do it?

Charlie I can do it, John. The question is can you?

John says nothing.

Just play by the rules, okay. That's how the money's made. Relax. Go get a blow job. Bottom line. We're not evaluated on how *accurate* our reports are. We're evaluated and *paid* on how many loans we make.

John But then loans for millions of dollars are being approved on reports –

Charlie Are you a moron? Or are you just out to piss me off? The committee doesn't approve a loan on the basis of a *report*. The committee approves a loan because if they *don't*, another bank *will*.

John Then why bother writing reports?

Charlie I'm not saying they don't *look* at it. I'm saying me and you play less of a role in this thing than you think.

John Then why are you asking me to manip—

Charlie Be careful now. Be *very* careful. Do you want to use that word? Do you want to say that word *aloud*? Let me tell you something first. About the power of words. You know, the Egyptians believed that speaking and writing was an act of creation. That when they spoke something aloud or wrote it down they brought it into being. It became *real*. And though crazy, we haven't really moved on from that. We do not speak of what we fear lest we bring it into being. We speak of our hopes as often as we can. To speak is to create. So think *very fucking carefully* about what you're about to create.

SEVEN

New York. John's apartment.
  John stands frozen, keys in hand.
  Frank, fifties, in 1950s clothing. He has two red dice.

John What are you doing?

Frank Surprise.

John What are you doing here?

Frank I was in the area . . .

  John says nothing.

It's good to see you.

  John still says nothing, he appears almost paralysed.

I was passing by and . . .

John How long have you been here?

Frank You've no toilet paper.

John What?

Frank I needed the john. Don't worry, I improvised.

He rolls the dices.

How's your mother? How are you?

John Fine.

Frank You look like shit. You've been away?

John What do you want?

Frank See my son . . .
It's a bad time. I can see it's a bad time. Like I said,
I was just passing by. I'll come back later. Another time. I
should've . . .

John Sit down. Just . . . sit down.

*

John and Frank shoot dice and drink together.

Frank This place needs some greenery. Oxygen. Plants.

John I don't like plants.

Frank What do you mean you . . .?

John They always die.

Frank If you don't look after them, they do.

John I don't want to have to look after things no more.

Frank So get cacti.

John I won't be here all that much anyway.

Frank This new job of yours?

John It's not just a job. It's a phenomenon.

Frank A phenomenon, huh?

John The fastest growing industry on earth, and I'm smack in the middle of it.

Frank What does a phenomenon do?

John I make loans to foreign governments and companies.

Frank You trust foreigners?

John I calculate the risk. You can always find alarming things to say about a third-world country . . . and there are alarming things. But it's important to look beyond the problems and see the possibilities. In Brazil we could be putting electricity in homes for the first time. It's like we're bringing the third world into the twentieth century.

Frank And what do you get out of it, what's your edge?

John We charge a fee, receive interest, like any bank. That's just the price of using someone else's money . . .
My first trip out and I'm shaking hands with the Brazilian Minister of Finance. That evening I'm at a cocktail party at the American Embassy exchanging business cards. When I got back to the hotel I ordered a seven dollar milkshake . . .

Frank Seven dollars.

John From room service.

Frank For a *milkshake*?

John For a milkshake.

Little pause.

Frank Tell me about this milkshake. What flavour?

John What do you mean, 'What flavour?'

Frank Cherry vanilla?

John Cherry vanilla.

Frank Better than Lexington's?

John *Come on.*

Frank For seven dollars . . .!

John There's Lexington's . . . and there's everybody else.

Frank (*with pride*) Lexington's is better than the Hilton, huh?

John It was good. Silky.

Frank Not too much ice.

John Or too much cherry.

Frank Chilled glass, heap of cream.

John No whipped cream.

Frank Seven dollars and no whipped cream? *Fuck that.*

John It was good, alright.

Frank Fuck that milkshake.

John It's my milkshake.

Little pause.

Frank You like the fellas you work with?

John They're great. Smart. Ivy League, all of them.

Frank You sure about that? Plenty of forged diplomas out there.

John They didn't forge their diplomas.

Frank I'm just saying . . .

John They wear the right clothes. They say the right things. They have good hair . . .
They don't have to fake, they're winners.

Frank And you fit in with that?

John Sure I fit in. Why would I not fit in?

Frank I'm just asking . . .

John If I didn't fit in I wouldn't have gotten this far. I've *earned* my place . . .

You know how hard it is, if you're *not* Ivy League? If you don't come from Long Island and play lacrosse on weekends? You don't just mail a résumé to these places. I worked in a back office, my existence unacknowledged. But I worked hard, harder than anybody else . . .

I don't always get their jokes. They speak fast. Think fast . . . I should get a television. I'd be able to talk about *Dallas*.

Frank When I was in jail I didn't make one friend. Not that I was short of offers, I was something of a celebrity to them. But I kept to myself. I'd play a role, join in; swap war stories. But we had nothing in common. They were in there for being dumb. I was in there for being smart. They made their money with a gun. I made mine with a telephone.

He sees his boasting has turned John away from him.

You still play the horn?

John You know I don't.

Frank But you still have it?

John You know I don't.

Frank If I knew I wouldn't be asking.

John You want another beer?

Frank You hocked it?

John Yeah, I hocked it.

Frank I bought you that horn.

John (*disbelief*) We needed the money!

Little pause.

Frank We should go sometime, see some jazz. That place still there?

Little pause.

John What place?

Frank That club, corner of Spring and . . . You know the place?

John You're planning on sticking around?

Frank I've got some business lined up.

John Business.

Frank Real estate. Selling real estate. Some feller inside, his brother –

John You're a salesman now?

Frank You and me both.

John I'm not a *salesman*.

Frank Your hairline's receding.

John I'm a *banker*.

Frank Ten years till the comb-over.

John And I'm not receding.

Frank (*adjusts his own hair*) We're more alike than you think.

John You don't know the first thing about me.

Pause.

Tell me about this job.

Frank I start Monday. Straight-up commission. Here's your cards, here's your brochures, there's the door . . .

John Real or fake?

Frank You don't believe me?

John I want to believe you.

Frank Real. What about yours?

EIGHT

Washington DC. Sheraton Hotel. Revolving doors.
A Hostess greets John and Charlie with a big smile and hands them a brochure.

Hostess Welcome to the annual meeting of the International Monetary Fund and World Bank.

Charlie Stop panting.

John I'm not panting.

Charlie You're panting.

John She's hot.

Charlie Does your lack of charisma concern you?

John (*reads the brochure*) 'How to alleviate third-world poverty . . .'

Charlie We're not here to listen to do-gooders talk poverty and development.

He bins the brochure.

Nobody is. We're here to make money . . . Welcome to the world's largest financial supermarket. Every loan officer across America is here. Along with the British, French, German, Japanese . . .

John There has to be thousands of us.

Charlie Everybody's got chips in this game. Best game in town.

Third-world delegates wearing colourful robes stream through . . .

Every third-world country on the planet is here for one weekend only. And they are gagging for credit. I can do more loans here in two days than in two months' worth of trips . . . Stop looking around like that. You look like a shoplifter. Okay, here we go: two o'clock.

John looks subtly.

See the blue badge? That's what we're here for.

John Blue badges?

Charlie Ministers of Finance.

John Who's that?

Charlie Finance Minister of South Africa, trying to convince the world his country isn't fucked. So this is how we hunt, we go after the ministers first; we book in an appointment – Okay, here we go, let's move . . .

John struggles to keep up with an excited Charlie.

I'll do the talking. Fuck . . .

John looks over: the Minister in question is no longer alone . . .

Banker 1 Patrick Lane, Morgan Stanley. How *are* you?

Minister Fine, thank you. Excuse me, I must use the bathroom.

Banker 1 Fan*ta*stic, I'm headed over there myself.

Charlie Three years ago Peru's a backwater . . .

John Now the oil's flowing, transforming his balance of payments –

Charlie (*unappreciative of the interruption*) You know, you really need to pay someone to shine your shoes. Three times a week – at least . . .

31

Green badges. Third-world delegates. If they're
well placed they can buttonhole you a meeting with a
minister . . . Grip and grin . . .

He shakes someone's hand . . .

Good to see you . . .

And another.

Here's my card . . .

And another.

We should get together . . .

John What about orange?

Charlie Journalists. Ignore them. Your focus is on deals.
When you're not talking to a minister, you're watching
who is. You need to be asking yourself what terms is
Qatar offering Poland? What's Kuwait saying to Argentina?
Because make no mistake, what the Arabs are asking
themselves is why let the West make all this profit from
recycling our petrodollars? When we could be doing it
ourselves . . .

This is the world stage, John, and you could be a
player on it . . . How's that report coming along? The
power plant.

Little pause.

John Good. Almost there.

Charlie Good . . .

Every once in a while Howard likes to bring someone
like you into the fold. Not because he believes in the
value of meritocracy or anything. No, he believes in the
value of being poor. He thinks it creates a special
determination . . .

Welcome aboard.

NINE

Sheraton Hotel. Continuous. A lavish party.

Banker 1 Philippines, *the* best place on earth to do business.

Banker 2 Martial Law has made it so much nicer, the security problems have *literally* vanished.

Banker 1 Not a bungalow in Makati without six servants.

Banker 2 Hostess bars are pretty good too.

Rick and Philip have joined Charlie and John.

Philip I hate to admit it, but they wear Brooks Brothers well, the Arabs.

Charlie You mean, Armani.

Philip Forgive me, I've crossed twelve time zones. I'm confused.

Rick Never mind the suits, where's the skirt? I thought this was a party.

Charlie This isn't a party, this is hell.

John (*raising his glass*) *This* is hell to you?

Charlie Everywhere is hell to me.

Trent Charlie?

Trent appears.

Charlie Trent. Trent. Good to . . .

Trent Guys.

Charlie See you. God when, when was it . . . ?

Trent Buenos Aires.

Charlie Buenos Aires. That must've been . . . ?

33

Trent Three years ago.

Charlie How *have* you been?

Trent Since your cocktail of Xanax and Halcion?

  Charlie laughs. Trent laughs. They stop laughing.

Charlie You and I both know I had nothing to do with that.

Trent You paid that hooker to slip it in my drink.

Charlie Now why would I . . . ?

Trent I was this close to clinching that loan.

Charlie The client felt differently.

Trent Who as it happens is now *your* client.

Charlie You can't seriously believe . . .

Trent What's it matter? Three years ago . . . in our industry that's a lifetime, we age in dog years. Hard to believe I've only been at Morgan five years. Few months back I started getting itchy feet. But then they made me Vice President.

Charlie (*with all the required fakery*) Congratulations.

Trent Latin American division. I can't tell you how much we're lending over there.

Charlie I'm sure you'll try.

Trent Let's put it this way, I'm personally responsible for two billion of it.

  Little pause.

Charlie Billion?

Rick *Two billion dollars?*

Philip That's impossible.

Rick How is that possible?

Trent In less than four years.

Rick Jesus Christ.

Trent Only at twenty-eight, I'm younger.

He slaps Charlie on the back and leaves.

Philip Imagine what his brokering account looks like.

Rick Imagine what their exposure is.

Charlie It's not our job to imagine . . . vast abstractions like the world economy.

TEN

Sheraton Hotel. Continuous.
John is getting a fresh drink at the bar. A beautiful display of tulips is there.

Grace They're from Holland.

John looks at the woman beside him.

The tulips. They fly them in for the conference.

John I didn't know that.

Grace Why would you?

John Excuse me?

Grace Can anyone tell the difference between a Dutch and an American tulip?

John A lot of money for someone to not notice.

Grace That gives you confidence someone will?

John Are you the decorator?

Grace Economic theory says that confidence is rational.

John You're not the decorator.

Grace But we ignore the obvious, what we know to be rationally true, when we're trusting. Confidence is often irrational. (*Extends hand.*) Grace.

John John.

Grace You're nervous, John.

John Not at all.

Grace Too hard a handshake, always a giveaway. You're a banker.

John How'd you guess?

Grace The suit. Brooks Brothers, right?

She offers him a cigarette; he declines.

Shouldn't you be pursuing a minister of finance?

John I'm . . . taking a breather.

Grace First time here?

John As a matter of fact, yes.

Grace Enjoying yourself?

John Absolutely. You?

Grace It's not the creepiest party I've been to. That would be my dad's fiftieth birthday. Greek-themed, he and his friends were Spartans. But it's a close second . . .
You don't look like you're enjoying yourself.

John You don't look like an economist.

Grace I never said I was.

John So, what are you doing here?

Grace Waiting for something to happen beyond my expectations . . .

John You're in the right place . . .

Grace (*flirtatiously direct*) Am I?

John I'll do more deals here in two days than in two months of trips abroad.

Grace That's confident. For a first-timer.

John It's my first time here but I have experience.

Grace You can't be a day older than twenty-four.

John In our work, we age in dog years.

Grace That sounds like something someone else would say.

John It's just an expression.

Grace It's just an observation.

John Maybe I've reason to be confident. As it happens, I just got back from Brazil . . .

Grace Saõ Paulo is the new Manhattan.

John And landed one of the biggest loans in our international portfolio.

Grace That must be quite a loan.

John Three hundred and twenty million . . .

Grace That is a sizeable loan.

John I mean, it wasn't just me. I didn't play that big a role.

Grace I'm a woman: self-deprecation's a language I understand.

John No, really, it wasn't just me. It was practically a done deal anyway. The Brazilians and my client are on friendly terms. Connections . . . what Latin America's all about.

Grace Who's your client?

John An American businessman.

Grace What's the loan for?

John Oh, uh, nuclear power plant.

Grace Where'd you say it was again?

John I didn't. What did you say you do again?

Grace I'm a journalist.

She hands him her card.

I'm good at what I do and I'm embarrassingly well connected.

He offers the card back.

Keep it.

John Aren't you supposed to wear a badge?

Grace I took it off.

John I don't think you're supposed to do that.

Grace I know. *Shh.*

John looks around for Charlie.

Five more minutes until the fireworks.

John Fireworks? Why fireworks?

Grace Why fireworks . . . ? Why orchestras? Why ice sculptures? To not see the spectre that's haunting the party.

End of Act One.

No interval.

Act Two

ONE

The Bank. 1979.
  Rick and Philip, feet up; reading the Wall Street Journal *and broadsheets.*

Philip We don't argue, and have sex once a week. That's our deal.

Rick Call her at lunch and tell her you're sorry.

Philip How do you know I'm to blame? You don't know what we were fighting about.

Rick Do you?
  So call her and say sorry.

Philip I hate it when we fight. That look of hers.

Rick She has a look? What's the look?

Philip Like she's disappointed. In me.

Rick Call her at lunch, tell her you're sorry. Ask me about Dana.

Philip How's Dana?

Rick Chanting.

Philip *Chanting?*

Rick She's gone Buddhist.

Philip Since when?

Rick Her move to the Hamptons.

Philip Why is it every woman that's had three dates with you goes on to crave depth?

Rick Depth?

Philip Some form of spirituality.

Rick Wait. You think Caroline's melon addiction was about depth and spirituality?

Philip Isn't fasting a preparation of the self for a spiritual awakening?

John appears.

Rick (*to John*) Have you heard the latest?

Philip (*undeterred*) There's a pattern here, we have to look at it.

Rick The latest on Robert, I mean. He had *concerns*.

John Robert had concerns?

Philip *That's* the latest?

Rick That's the latest.

Philip That's *why* he left?

Rick *If* he left.

John Robert left?

Philip What kind of concerns?

Rick Our exposure in Latin America.

Philip This *is* Robert Fisher we're talking about, Vice President –

John Not any more.

Philip But *Robert* concerned about our *exposure*?

Rick He was going to be demoted, that's why he left.

Philip He *voiced* these concerns?

Rick This is what I heard.

Philip You think it's true?

Rick It's a rumour.

John But do you believe it?

Rick *Absolutely* not. That's not the point. The point is . . .

Philip What's the point?

Rick Rumours speak of fears . . .
You know left-handed people die younger. Five years on average.

John I'm right-handed.

Rick I'm relieved.

John leaves – a Banker is asleep in his chair. He picks up some papers.

John You snooze, you lose.

Banker keeps his eyes closed, gives John the middle finger.

Rick So . . . ?

Philip So . . . ?

Rick So Robert gone, who for Vice President?

Philip and Rick scope the room, eyes on Charlie.

Philip He's too young.

Rick How old is he?

Philip Twenty-eight? Thirty?

Rick He's not thirty. He told me he'd be dead before thirty.

Philip That's what all exceptional people say – or people that think they are – dead before thirty or immortality. Me and you, we'll go bald and get bunions.

Rick We're not exceptional?

Philip Two guys that got lucky . . .
I'm going to go call her now.

TWO

The Bank. Howard's office.
Howard's at his desk with his yo-yo in hand.

Howard When I was starting out – what? Thirty years ago? I asked Eric Walsh, legendary banker back then, what the key to his success was. One thing above all else, I ask. He thinks for a minute, then says to me, my umbrella.

John His umbrella?

Howard Every working day of his life, the man carried an umbrella. Didn't matter if there was a heatwave, he had this umbrella. I ask him why, and he says to me, 'Because every morning when I leave for the commuter train and every evening when I come home, the residents, the homemakers, look outside their windows, see me passing, and say to themselves, there's a *safe* pair of hands. There's a good bank.'

A little light laughter.

If you're not taking risks, you're not a bank. And if you're still relying on homemakers for growth . . . don't bother: domestic lending's grown four per cent. *Four per cent*. Our foreign earnings have grown seven times that. From seventeen to forty-nine per cent of total earnings . . .

I want to expand our international division. I want to triple our lending. Open up into territories unknown – Zaire, Uganda. I see the third world as a vast new California – one we've only just begun to mine. But the committee . . . the committee are men of the old tradition. Nervous nellies. Encyclopaedic knowledge of domestic banking, not a clue when it comes to foreign. To them foreign means volatile and risky – and that's just Alabama . . .

They had reservations about the Brazilian power plan. It was your report that pushed it through.

Howard looks straight at John.

John It's a safe bet, sir.

Howard Glad to hear it.

He gets back to his paperwork: the meeting's over.

John I hear Robert Fisher's left.

Howard looks up sharply; dangerously.

I thought that might mean Charlie would be getting promoted.

Howard says nothing.

Less available . . . maybe. To expand into new territories.

Howard sits back in his chair.

I thought there might be an opening. For me. For my own portfolio.

Pause.

Howard You ever make pancakes?

John Pancakes? Sometimes.

Howard It's a great mark of character.

John Making pancakes?

Howard How do you flip yours, John?

John I, er . . . well, I put the flour into the mixing –

Howard No, no. How do you flip your pancake?

Little pause.

John I give it a good flip, sir. Because if you don't, if you're timid, unwilling to risk your pancake, it will fly up a few inches but it won't turn over. But if you're reckless,

43

if you flip it too hard, it will go too high and end up on the floor.

Howard Just as I thought.

He resumes his paperwork: the meeting's over. John lingers for an extra uncertain for seconds before making to leave.

John? You've got yourself a slice of a portfolio – and a leash.

John Yes, sir.

Howard A short leash.

THREE

John's apartment block. Night.
John and Frank are drinking.

John They look at me differently now, guys I work with.

Frank Sure they do.

John I see them re-evaluate.

Frank People are shallow.

John Go back over their arithmetic, cross out the sum they had, add me up again.

Frank I've been up here and down there. I've had a hundred friends and I've had none. Your stock's risen, but know your own worth.

John I do.

Frank I was thinking earlier, you never hear of a Marvin nowadays. Where'd all the Marvins go? They were everywhere, on the street, in stores. And now – what? They die?

John They'll be back.

Frank They'll be back, huh? It all comes back, stick around long enough . . .

Yesterday, I'm on Broadway and 42nd and what do I see? The tat. You remember the tat? Crooked dice with fives on four sides . . .

John And sixes on two.

Frank Fleecing a crowd with the oldest con there is.

John It all comes back . . .

I ever tell you about my escape box? I had this box, shoe box, in the back of my closet. I had it . . . I don't know a year – maybe more – for when you came back. I was convinced you would. Escape somehow. I had some things in there I'd swiped from around the house. Few dollars. I'd bring it out at night, empty it, repack it. Some point I realised you weren't coming back. That I needed an escape plan of my own. I'd look at those skyscrapers in my room at night. I didn't know what happened in them but I knew they were important. Important buildings. Important people inside. I knew that they were my escape.

Little pause.

Frank I want to say something, but what?

John You don't have to say anything . . . I got here despite of it all.

Frank raises his bottle.

Frank To the good life.

John To the good life . . .

You remember Hannah Rogers? Haven't thought about her in years. Tonight I thought about calling her.

Frank Well, what about it?

John Call her? I don't have her number. It was just a . . . it was years – she wouldn't even remember who I was.

Frank She'll remember. Women remember. *Everything.* You think you're a guy people forget. You got to stop thinking like that. You're a salesman now and salesmen –

John I'm *not* a salesman.

Frank I thought you sold money?

John It's more complicated than that.

Frank Trust me, selling's complicated. They say yes only to evaporate three days later, I can't get the bastards on the phone. I say to myself, Mike Schmidt. Mike Schmidt failed at the plate two out of three times and still one of the greatest ball players of all time . . .

John Give me your pitch . . . pretend I'm on the other end of the phone.

Frank says nothing.

Come on. Give me the pitch, and I'll tell you where you're –

Frank I don't need your help, alright.

John I'm just saying if you want to get ahead, I can –

Frank I said I didn't need it.

Little pause.

John So where's all this money come from then, Frank? The whisky. The cigars.

Frank It's not that much.

John New suit.

Frank (*beams*) I wasn't sure you'd noticed the threads.

John I noticed. Where's it from?

Frank Brooks Brothers.

John I meant the money. Where's the money come from?

Frank I sold my first condo, alright.

John You just said you couldn't get the bastards back on the phone.

Frank I got one of them.

John Right.

Frank It only takes one.

John Then why didn't you tell me that?

Frank We were celebrating you. Your success, not mine. We're both doing better. How about that?

FOUR

Santiago, Chile. Lobby of a luxury hotel.
John and a Chilean businessman, maybe a bodyguard; secretary, walking . . .

John I'll speak to our New York office but I can't see any foreseeable problems.

Chilean It's been a pleasure.

John And thank you for coming here.

Chilean This hotel has many memories. My eldest daughter's wedding was here.

John Wow. That must have been . . .

Chilean Expensive. Tomorrow we will visit the construction site, yes?

John Sounds perfect.

Chilean Welcome to Chile, Mr Anderson.

They shake hands . . .
Grace appears – maybe she's at the reception desk – as the Chileans exit.
John hesitates, but finally goes for it as she leaves the reception desk.

John Hi, I . . . thought it was you.

Grace Sorry, do I . . . ?

John We've met before.

Grace I don't think so.

John Washington.

Grace Washington?

John The annual IMF/WB . . .

Grace The Sheraton?

John Right. We were at the bar.

Grace You look different.

John Oh yeah?

Grace You're not wearing glasses.

John I've never worn glasses.

Grace Really?

John Yes.

Grace I could've sworn –

John What are you doing here?

Grace A story.

John What's the story?

Grace The Chilean economic miracle.

John Actually, I've read some of your articles. They're good.

Grace Thanks.

John Well-written. Not that I agree with them.

Grace Not that you would.

John That piece on the Philippines . . . what was it?

Grace 'Philippines: the Pacific Powder Keg?' My editor put in the question mark.

John With growth at 6.5 per cent . . .?

Grace And I've already had this conversation with him.

John It's the safest bet in Asia.

Grace I'd ask what you're doing here but I can guess. How's it working out for you?

John Great. Couldn't be better.

Grace Well, great running into you, uh . . . Stephen?

John John.

Grace You'll have to excuse me.

She leaves, he hesitates, then blurts . . .

John You want to get some dinner later?

FIVE

Hotel restaurant on the beach, lots of twinkling lights. The sound of the ocean.
   Grace and John are between courses.

Grace You've never been to any of the sights?

John I spend my time in hotels, offices, taxis, restaurants . . .

Grace Tell me you've at least been for a walk.

John I get a different view. I see the country from the inside. Business, bureaucracy.

Grace Sounds riveting.

John I feel part of things.

Grace Your suit costs more than people here earn in a month.

John Not the people I meet.

Grace Tomorrow I'm going to Santa Lucia, Javier says the views are incredible.

John Javier?

Grace The bartender.

John You should be careful. Kidnappings are routine here.

Grace Under Pinochet, Chileans have a lot more to fear than us.

John There's plenty of time for sightseeing. Fifteen years from now I'll have retired.

Grace Is that right?

John I'll make a pile of money first.

Grace How much is that?

John Enough that it won't ever again be a problem.

Grace What if money becomes the problem?

John It won't.

Grace You can never be too rich or too thin, my mother says. She's very, very happy.

Pause.

How was money a problem?

John What?

Grace You said enough that it won't ever again be a problem.

Little pause.

John My father . . . was in jail. My mom raised me alone. Usually, I tell people he's dead.

Grace You tell people he's *dead*?

John It's just easier.

Grace Why, what did he do?

John Fraud.

Grace Oh . . . I thought you were going to say serial killer.

John You're not too disappointed, I hope.

Grace What kind of fraud?

John He was a small-time operator – though not to hear him talk. To hear him, he was a big fish. Everything about him was big. His laugh. Appetite. Gifts he bought. Parties he threw. Growing up, it never occurred to me that it was all fake. He was a hot air balloon, this magical thing that lifted you up, and burnt you . . .

I don't really want to talk about it. I don't know why I . . . I just didn't want to lie about it this time. I don't have to do that any more. I've succeeded where he failed . . . How's the wine?

She acknowledges it's good.

This is how you live a life . . .

So if you're sightseeing tomorrow that mean you've finished your story?

Grace The Chilean miracle?

John You say it like you don't believe in miracles.

Grace Well, private debt is soaring.

John Before Pinochet inflation was over a *thousand* per cent, it's now thirty.

Grace I think the miracle's fuelled by debt.

John The modern world's fuelled by debt.

Grace These levels are unsustainable.

John The best economists in the world happen to disagree.

Grace They're being paid to be consensus.

John Can we talk about something else?

Grace They all share the same world view.

John Speaking of which, we have this fabulous view to enjoy.

Grace Your bank's been increasing its loan portfolio by twenty-five per cent each year.

John Countries are taking advantage of low interest rates, as they should.

Grace You see no problem with them acquiring mountains of debt?

John Growth takes care of debt.

Grace Is three dollars of debt to create one dollar of growth sustainable?

John It's not the size of a country's debt that matters, it's whether they can service it.

Grace But if they're earning one dollar for three dollars of debt . . . ?

John And all our loans are being serviced.

Grace By new loans . . . right? Extend and pretend.

John doesn't answer; instead he pours more wine.

How else are they supposed to pay back money they don't have?

John Latin American economies have the highest growth rates *in the world*.

Grace Oh, I've seen those double digits too.

John They're growing. Long term, their growth will easily outpace their debt.

Grace See, when I look at a country like Brazil, I see these huge debt-financed projects that aren't bringing in

any revenue. The money's clearly being squandered –
the Ferrovia railroad, Transamazonica highway, Tucurui
dam . . . they have power plants eighty miles west of Rio
that aren't even operational. In fact, wasn't it your bank
that did the loan . . . ?

John Is this why you came to dinner? Ask me questions.
Find your next story.

Grace I don't need to ask. I can tell you the story, if
you'd like.

John The credit system is sound. And the idea that you, a
journalist – forgive me a woman nobody's basically heard
of – knows more than the world's leading economists,
than the World Bank, the IMF, the Fed, every financial
news outlet, rating agencies, not to mention the hundreds
of credit analysts at the banks themselves . . . the idea
you know something they don't is . . .

He laughs, she doesn't react; he stops laughing.

I'm sorry, but the idea's absurd.

Grace What's absurd is behaving as if the biggest credit
bubble in history doesn't exist.

John Well, it's pretty hard to see what's not there.

Grace Especially when you're being paid not to . . .
    You know, the word credit is from the Latin *credere* to
believe. All this debt, it just maintains a fiction.

John It's not a fiction.

Grace You're rescheduling reality. You can't do that for
ever.

John We're developing these countries and that costs
money.

Grace Developing? I thought you were propping up
dictators, like Pinochet.

John Pinochet's not a dictator.

Grace Not a dictator? You know how the state police here deal with political dissidents? Trade unionists, students, you know, that type? They sew live rats into their vaginas. They die from the starved rat trying to get out. From the ripping and tearing.

She stands.

Enjoy your steak.

She leaves.
   He listens to the sound of the ocean. It sounds unreal.

SIX

Hotel bar on the beach. Later that night. The sound of the ocean.
   John has been drinking heavily.

John Hey . . .

The Bartender wearily polishes glasses.

Hey . . . same again.

The Bartender pours one from the bottle.

Keep going . . . keep . . . that's it.

The Bartender resumes polishing.

It's Javier, right?

Bartender *Si, señor.*

John You've worked here long?

Bartender Six years.

John Wow.

Bartender It's not so long.

John A hamster's life span is three.

Bartender I would like to leave.

John You should do that.

Bartender Open my own bar.

John You should definitely do that.

Bartender No bank will give me credit.

Little pause.

John I'm not a retail banker.

Bartender Retail . . . ?

John I don't *do* mortgages, car loans, small business . . .

Bartender (*placating*) *Si, señor.*

John I do *big* business. That's what I do.

Bartender *Si, señor.*

John It's because of me, because of what I *do*, that the poorest people in this country will have clean water. But not without credit. With interest rates this low, money's never been so cheap, it's practically free.

Bartender I come from a small village, Niebla. A fishing village. Long way from here. Women sell shrimp under palm trees. Men go out on small boats. Nothing much happens. Then one day the ocean went away. Like a sheet pulled from a bed. Whoosh, it was gone. Everybody came to see the empty beach. Empty but for fish. The ocean had left them behind! Fish trapped in puddles of water everywhere. A miracle. The villagers brought the priest to thank the Lord. Fish for everyone, free fish for a year! The women fill their skirts. Men fill their nets. Children help too. Most of them do not hear the first shake of the ground, they are too busy. The second shake, everyone hears it. They stop and look and they see . . . a wall. A huge wall moving towards them. A black wall. A wall of water. Baskets are dropped. Children are grabbed. People are running, screaming. But the wall is too fast. Too high. It is too late . . . they all die.

Where I come from, *señor*, we don't believe in miracles.
Everything has its price . . .

John has left the bar, and stumbles out on to the beach.
    *He bumps into a silhouetted couple walking hand in
hand.*

John Sorry.

He bumps into another silhouetted figure.

Sorry.

He retches.

(*To no one.*) Sorry. Sorry.

*He collapses on to a sun lounger, is sick on the floor
and passes out . . .*
    *He wakes to two Security Guards surveying him,
one is holding his wallet.*

Security 1 Mr Anderson?

John (*confused*) What?

Security 1 Mr Frank Anderson?

John No. That's not me.

Security Guard 2 takes the wallet and reads.

Security 2 Frank Anderson?

John That's not me.

Security 1 Mr Frank Anderson?

John No, no –

Security 2 Who are you?

John That's not –

Security 1 Do you know who you are?

John That's not me, that's not me, that's –

SEVEN

John's apartment.
    Frank is drinking champagne and smoking a fat cigar.

Frank Life is habit-forming. This was one of my epiphanies inside: form good habits.

John What happened here?

Frank I had a little party, few friends –

John The place is a mess.

Frank I'll clean up tomorrow.

John And I don't want you smoking that in here.

Frank Relax, will you?

John What is all this stuff?

Frank Get yourself a glass.

John I don't want a drink. We're drinking too much.

Frank We've earned our place in the good life.

    John picks up another empty bottle.

John Have you been drinking all day?

    Frank says nothing.

Why aren't you in the office?

    Frank laughs.

What?

Frank There is no office.

John What'd you mean, there's no office?

Frank There's *no* office. There's a brass plate outside. No office.

John But . . . you said there was?

Frank I lied.

John You *lied?*

Frank says nothing.

Why?

Frank Why'd you think?

John I don't know. I don't . . .

Frank Sure you do.

John's confusion gives way to horror.

John Because it's fake . . . a scam . . .

Frank It's a classier outfit than that but . . .

John You're unbelievable.

Frank A man's got to make a living.

John What is wrong with you?!

Frank Hey, I'm only taking for myself what life refused to give me.

John How could you?

Frank It was simple enough, what can I tell you? People are dumb.

People want something for nothing, alright. That's human nature. Only you can't get something for nothing. But it's their desire for it that leads them to men like me. What did I always tell you? You can't cheat an honest man. I make no apologies for my life, for what I do, and if that's what you're expecting . . .

In this game, the day you're sorry, is the day you're dead in the water.

John Sorry? *Sorry?* I don't expect you to say *sorry*. Why would you? You never gave a fuck about me, about Mom –

Frank That's not true.

John About anybody but yourself. *Yes, it is true.* Mom lost *everything*.

Frank Let's not go back there –

John No, you're going to listen to this!

Frank Its history, John –

John She lost everything! The house, car, savings, every stick of furniture, every friend, *everything and everyone* because of you, and one little fucking word cannot apologise for that.

Frank She knew what she was getting into. She never asked but she knew.

John Don't you dare –

Frank Your mother had certain expectations, lifestyle requirements. And while ever she was getting the furs, the jewellery –

John How fucking dare you –

Frank Everybody was having a good time out it, and then the shit hit the fan, and everybody turns to me, and *nobody* takes any personal responsibility –

John *You committed fraud!* You robbed people of their *entire life's savings.* Mom had nothing to do with it but she had to pay for it. She served your sentence. She was left with your debts, debts that you racked up: eighty thousand in back taxes, twenty thousand from credit lines you took out and blew on *what*?! Whores! Wheels! Good times – She took two jobs, she worked day and night paying off debts, debts that you knew, that you . . . that you knew . . . debts that . . .

Frank What's a matter, John? You look like you've seen a ghost.

John Get out.

Frank I lost a lot too, you know –

John GET OUT.

John forces Frank out of the door . . . slams it shut.

EIGHT

The Bank. Elevator, going up.
   Rick and Philip, coats on, newspapers, standing either side of John.

Rick I woke up this morning and had this feeling . . .

Philip What feeling?

Rick That it had all happened before.

Philip We're growing old in airports.

   John sees the elevator light flicker. Rick and Philip remain oblivious.

Rick That's the thing with repetition . . .

Philip It's spiritually disastrous?

Rick It surrenders us to inevitability.

   Little pause.

Philip Ask me about the traffic in Cairo.

Rick How's the traffic in Cairo?

Philip Impressive.

Rick More impressive than Tehran?

Philip More impressive than even Tehran.

Rick What about the heat?

Philip Fatal. Heat's fatal.

   Little pause.

How was Venezuela?

Rick They prefer Pepsi to Coke.

Philip Huh. Who knew?

John sees the elevator light flicker, again no reaction from Rick and Philip.

Rick You know turtles can breathe through their assholes?

Philip No. I didn't know that.

Rick And seals . . .

Philip What about seals?

Rick It's not unknown for them to screw penguins.

Philip What were you watching last night?

Rick Documentaries.

Philip I watched a movie but fell asleep, now I want to know how it ends.

Rick He dies.

Philip You watched it?

Rick Nope.

Philip So how'd you know how it ends?

Rick All plots essentialise down to death.

Ding! Rick and Philip step out the elevator.
John steps out the elevator and walks through the bank: a hive of activity, dialling, redialling, telexes, and people. The dial of the world's sound is turned up just a touch – like a hungover experience where everything is a shade brighter and louder.
Charlie appears, on the move.

Charlie I want to spend the night in a trauma unit, I want to plunge my fist into a chest cavity and see the flat blue line spike into life; resuscitate the dead, cure the mad, able the disabled, somebody show me my *fucking limits* . . .
Where have you been?

John I had something to deal with.

Charlie You were due back yesterday.

John Something important.

Charlie Making money's not important? You look like shit.

John I haven't slept much, I –

Charlie The less you talk, the better you'll feel.

John I need a coffee –

Charlie I need you right here.

He is signing off some file handed to him by a staffer.

Leave them in my office.

John Your office?

The staffer nods in the direction.

Robert's office?

Staffer Vice President.

John Congratulations.

Charlie For Vice Presidency? I'm twenty-eight. What'd you expect?

John When'd this happen?

Howard appears . . .
The floor quietens as he strides to the front.

Howard Less than an hour ago, the Shah of Iran was forced to flee his country.

Surprise reactions . . .

Needless to say, though there's been some protests and unrest over there, nobody saw this coming. But we do see what happens next: chaos. And chaos in Iran means world's oil prices are about to rocket. For those of you who weren't around five years ago to see the last oil crisis . . . the world is about to change. But with every crisis comes opportunity . . .

As of today, I am expanding our international division and we are tripling our lending. We were right to lend what we did in '73 and 1979 will go down as the year we were right again . . .

This is your opportunity. Your time to sell, sell, sell. So smile and dial, boys. Do you hear that? It's the roar of money . . .

Whirlwind of excited activity – out of the mix appears Frank by the window.

Frank Nice view.

John is too stunned to respond.

Long way down. Anybody jump?

John You can't be here.

Frank The art of the con is in its fluidity . . . like a lulling current, it pulls you along.

John You can't be here.

Frank Seduces you . . .

John looks around panicked, but no one reacts to Frank's presence.

A beautiful thing to be inside.

John Don't think I don't know what you're doing.

Frank There's so much to learn, John.

John You're trying to destroy me because I am everything you are not.

Frank We'd make quite a team, sport.

John I'm calling security.

Frank Together, the sky's the limit!

Charlie John?

John You need to leave *now*.

Charlie John?!

John, flustered, turns to Charlie.

What are you doing?

John It's fine, he's leaving.

Charlie What?

John It won't happen again.

Charlie What are you talking about?

John I can get rid of him.

Charlie Who?

John sees that Charlie does not see Frank . . .

Rid of who?

That nobody sees Frank but him.

Charlie What the fuck is going on?

End of Act Two.

Interval.

Act Three

ONE

The Bank. 1982.
Philip and Rick, feet up, reading Euromoney *and the* Wall Street Journal.

Philip I wish I was a dolphin. Fucking around in the sea all day.

Rick (*reading*) Warner's saying the Fed's lowering interest rates.

Philip I swear, every fucking time he says that, they go up.

Rick At eighteen per cent, they can't go any higher.

Philip It doesn't mean they're going down either.

He starts eating something sugary, colourful and nasty.

Rick Its eight a.m., how can you eat that?

Philip I need comforting.

Rick What's wrong?

Philip My life.

Rick Is that all? Everything okay with you and Clarissa?

Philip Everything's great.

Rick Nothing's wrong with . . . ?

Philip Kids are fine.

Rick So . . . ?

Philip So . . . I don't know. It's just . . . I have this feeling, this . . .
Why am I telling you this?

65

Rick You see redemption in my eyes.

Philip I'm not telling you this.

Philip gets back to reading.

Rick You live a fully executed life and yet something's missing . . .

Philip lowers the paper.

You feel this. Not only do you feel it, you probably know what it is . . .

The light draws gradually around Philip, until only his head is lit.

It's inside of you. But it's become unavailable. Sealed off. Like the contents of a jar you just can't open however many times you try. And you did try, didn't you? You offered your jar to someone else. Someone of the opposite sex. Watched helplessly as they tried to unscrew it, got frustrated, and gave up. And you accepted, with a little detached irony, your own condition. This does not mean you don't experience the sublime in the secular, that joy does not dance out of you . . .

Your days are work-filled. You read the news. The stain of world events imprinted on finger and thumb. The data stream pulses. And you doubt the reality of any of it. In such moments, you feel the physical presence of a force unknown. You reach for the cosmological . . .

You find yourself in the science section of a bookshop, thumbing physics. Atoms, neutrons, gravity, matter: all of it incomprehensible. Unemployment's topping out at ten, interest rates are up to twenty, inflation at thirteen, and the Fed's not backing down . . .

You do something different. Something you haven't done in a while. You take the subway. The air-conditioning surprises you. The number of people talking to themselves, the low mutter of the mad, does not. The dollar bills in your wallet reassure. The lights go epileptic, and barrelling into the dark it hits you. You are a speck of dust charging through the cold black . . .

It's 1982 and already you're tired of this decade.

The light pops wide.

Philip It's probably a common experience . . .
I've started exfoliating.

Rick How's that working out for you?

Philip Better. Thanks.

He takes his feet off his desk and looks at his screen.

Are you getting this?

Rick *Closed?*

Philip Doesn't make any sense . . .

Rick Hey, Charlie?

Charlie walking past –

Philip Mexico's foreign exchange markets are closed?

Charlie Closed?

Philip Reuters wire: 'Mexican government closes its foreign exchange.'

Charlie When'd this . . . ?

Philip Now.

Charlie They say why?

Philip No, just . . .

Charlie Doesn't make any sense . . .

Philip You don't close an exchange unless . . .

Charlie Let's hold the panic.

Philip Except you don't close an exchange *unless* there's a panic.

Rick Isn't John down in Mexico?

Howard Charlie?

He is out of his office and on the move.

What's going on?

Charlie Mexico's closed its foreign –

Howard My question is *why*?

Charlie Obviously they're stopping anyone from changing pesos into dollars. Not that I see any compelling reason for them to have to hoard dollars. The peso's overvalued, we know this, but nothing that can't be weathered . . .

Howard I see. So your answer is you don't know.

Little pause.

Charlie Right.

Howard nods, walks away.
 Rick and Philip.

Philip Maybe now's an appropriate time for us to go to the men's room.

Rick The men's room?

Philip It's where we regain control of the world.

TWO

Mexico. The Minister's office.
 The Minister's Secretary and John. She has fixed him a drink.

John You're not joining me?

Secretary I don't drink in the afternoon.

John What about in the evening?

Secretary I'm married.

John Even better. Where would you like to go? I can get us a table anywhere.

Minister appears. He and the Secretary exchange a few words, and she leaves.

Minister Thank you for waiting, Mr Anderson.

John Not at all. I've been well taken care of . . . New secretary?

Minister (*distracted*) What?

John I said, new secretary?

Little pause.

Minister You do not know.

John Know what?

Minister I see . . .

The Minister is quiet again, ashen.

John Are you okay?

Minister This heat . . . perhaps we take off our jackets. Formalities.

John I'm no stickler for formality.

Minister Today we can do away with it. I know why you are here. You are here to offer me a loan. But you are not really lending me money. You are the person you are lending to.

John I'm not sure I follow –

Minister All these loans never leave your bank, the money never leaves New York. No money actually changes hands. But your statements show paper profits and my debt goes up. That *is* real.

John I'm not sure what you're getting at.

Minister Interest rates. They too, are real. Eighteen per cent. Every point increase adds billions to our debt service.

John Interest rates will go down.

Minister When?

John I don't need to tell you what the unemployment figures are back home.

Minister Your Federal Reserve is waging war on American inflation and killing us

John You've had cheap money for a decade – and you were right to take advantage of it.

Minister Precisely what every single expert who came to this country told us. For Mexico, the sky was the limit. We would build twenty new cities, four new ports, power stations, a new national gas grid . . . Mexico would become France.

John What you have done is develop a lucrative oil industry . . .

Minister And it cost twenty billion to do so. It takes a lot of money to industrialise, Mr Anderson. So you see, it is very easy to run up an eighty billion dollar tab.

Little pause.

John Eighty billion?

Minister Give or take.

John What . . . what are you saying?

Minister Mexico is bankrupt.

John is stunned into silence.

You are our largest creditor, this is why I am telling you this now.

John What do you mean, *bankrupt*?

Minister I mean we are out of money. Tomorrow I will have told Washington and our other creditors the same thing. You know J. Paul Getty once said, if you owe a hundred dollars to the bank, it's your problem. If you owe a hundred million, it's the bank's problem. Tomorrow I will tell them, when its eighty billion you owe . . . it's everybody's problem.

THREE

The Bank. Howard's office.
John, Charlie, Howard.

Howard How does a country go bankrupt and you not be privy to it?

John (*indignant*) Every rating agency had it as a top bet till two days ago!

Howard How many times have you been to Mexico these last six months?

John (*defensive*) Me personally? I'm not sure . . . three?

Howard *Four.* I read your reports last night. (*To Charlie.*) I read *everybody's*.

Charlie Howard, there really was no way of knowing –

Howard Are you trying to tell me that a country can go bankrupt in *secret*?! This shit storm's been brewing for months and every goddamned Sanchez on the street knew

71

it, since the smart money's been fleeing the country!
Meanwhile, you're throwing in American checking and
savings accounts.

Charlie Mistakes were made.

*John turns to Charlie, stunned – and pissed – at this
concession.*

Howard No. Fucking. Kidding.

L. B. Holmes enters.

Howard Charlie Hewitt, Vice President. John Anderson,
Assistant Vice President.

*Holmes briefly acknowledges them and unloads her
files.*

L. B. Holmes.

Charlie What's the L?

John Linda?

Charlie Laura?

John Lucy?

Holmes Lawyer.

Holmes takes a seat.

In the event of a Mexican default –

John Whoa. *Default?*

Charlie I think we're getting ahead of ourselves –

Howard If Mexico defaults, this bank is going to the
wall.

John They're not going to default.

Holmes If they can't meet their interest payments –

Charlie Which is why we need to give them more loans, roll over the existing debt . . .

Howard No more loans.

Little pause.

Charlie No more loans?

Howard I'm not throwing any more good money after bad.

Charlie How else can they keep up their interest payments?

Howard There's plenty of banks –

John There isn't a bank in the world that will lend to Mexico right now!

Holmes Maybe I should start with the loan agreements?

Charlie (*appealing*) Howard, those agreements protect us –

Holmes Actually, they're worthless.

Charlie Trust me, they're not worthless.

Holmes I wouldn't trust you to run a hot dog stand.

Charlie You want to know what the world's leading economists think about Mexico? What the World Bank, the IMF thought just nine weeks ago? I can tell you because I have their reports right here. (*Reads.*) 'There is *considerable scope for sustained additional borrowing . . .*'

Holmes I wouldn't trust them either.

John The Mexicans lied to us! They lied.

Howard Let's get back to the loan agreements.

Holmes Should Mexico miss an interest payment –

Charlie (*we know this tone*) The loan goes straight into default, giving us the legal right to make the loan due and payable in full right there –

Holmes Except Mexico's not a bankrupt steel mill. You can't force a sovereign country into liquidation. And if you can't force it to liquidate, you can't sell its assets in order to pay back your loans –

Howard So what can we do?

Holmes As Mexico's biggest creditor . . . watch. Watch

Pause.

Howard Everything stops. Everything. There are no more new loans to Latin America –

John What?!

Charlie Howard?

John Okay. Brazil is not Mexico.

Howard We don't know what it is, and until we do –

John Venezuela is not Mexico, Argentina is not Mexico, Chile is not –

Charlie Now is not the time to be shrinking our portfolio.

John Shrinking? It's having its balls cut off.

Charlie We have led the way in the debt market, and now you want to lead a retreat?

Howard I want you on planes first thing tomorrow and I want existing debts paid up.

Charlie Howard, these relationships have taken years to develop –

John Mexico's having problems, that doesn't mean the rest of the South –

Howard I'm looking at balance sheets, and I don't even know what they mean any more.

John If you do this you'll set off a panic.

Howard When news of Mexico's insolvency spreads, then you'll see a panic.

John You're precipitating it! And for what? Has there been a run on Mexican banks? Has there been a social revolution? Nothing, nothing, has been destroyed. The system works. The system . . .

A roar of voices: shouts, exasperations, from outside. Philip storms in.

Philip Mexico's announced a ninety-day suspension on all interest payments . . .

The office strobe light blinks on and off.

It's defaulting.

The office light blinks off.
    John sees a Figure in a in a suit identical to his own appear before him.

Figure When man created the gun, for the first time he could kill, quicker than he could think. His thought process being slower than a bullet . . .
    Oh, and . . . *nice cuff links.*

The Figure recedes.

FOUR

A bar.
    Charlie and John are drinking heavily. Charlie cuts a despondent figure.

Charlie I'm not having fun any more.

He openly shovels cocaine up a nostril.

John What are you doing?

Charlie Obliterating reality with drink, drugs and, a couple of hours from now, sex. Not that there's anything to fuck here. (*Breathes.*) Life's so much easier with coke.

John shovels in the coke also.

John I think they drug the animals at the zoo.

Charlie What?

John The zoo. I think the animals are drugged.

Charlie You went to the zoo?

John It was the way they looked at me from their cages.

Charlie But . . . the zoo's in the Bronx?

Little pause.

John What the hell was that L. B. business anyway?

Charlie Howard came up with it is what I heard, it's how he got her past the board and hired.

John They signed off on it without knowing she was a woman?

Charlie Somebody's daughter no doubt.

John I need more drink . . . (*Looks for the waiter.*) This strategy, this, let's stop everything . . . We might as well hold the door wide open for our competitors. Just last month Morgan took out a full page advertising their increased lending. This whole thing is blown out of all proportion. Mexico is going to play by the rules.

Charlie Were we just in the same meeting?

John Where's the goddamn waiter?

Charlie They just told us to go fuck ourselves.

John They're buying some time. Ninety days. That's all they've asked for.

Charlie You think that was them *asking*?

John I think I need a drink . . .

John goes to the bar. A woman turns around: it's Grace.

Grace?

Grace It's been a while.

John It's . . . good to see you.

Grace Why do I not believe you?

John What are you doing here?

Grace I think we all need a drink right now, don't you?

John You've heard about Mexico, obviously. It's taken us all by surprise.

Grace Surprise? Well there's an indictment if I ever heard one.

John Look, if you're going to start –

Grace You knew. All you boys knew. You were just too busy getting rich to care.

John That's the story you want to tell, go ahead.

Grace No more stories. I quit.

John You quit?

Grace And I am *very* drunk.

John Why'd you quit?

Grace I wrote a piece on Morgan's exposure in Latin America, Morgan got wind of it. Their ad men called my editor, said, 'Listen, we really like your magazine but there's this story you're doing on our bank . . .' My editor killed the piece. So I quit. Hours later, the biggest story of my career breaks . . .

John My heart's bleeding.

Grace So what's the strategy?

John Strategy?

Grace You're Mexico's largest creditor, right?

John We're working on it.

Grace How much debt are you holding?

John You ask a lot of questions for someone that's quit.

Grace Get used to it. They'll all be asking questions now.

The light in the bar flickers.

Mexico is just the beginning.

Grace turns away.

John Since when did Mexico, *Mexico*, start dictating the rules of the game?

Charlie appears at the bar beside John.

Charlie The rules, it appears, are optional.

Grace is no longer at the bar.

We are not going to get a dime back of what they borrowed . . .

John What's a matter with you?

Charlie And if we're going to survive this – I'm not talking about the bank, fuck the bank. I'm talking about me and you. We need to be smart. They're going to want answers: the board, stockholders, everything we've ever done under a microscope . . .

John What are you talking about?

Charlie *Billions of dollars* are about to disappear.

John What do you mean, everything *we've* ever done?

Charlie What do you *think* I mean?

John We've done no different to anyone else.

Charlie That's not going to save our skin.

John Save? I've done what was expected of me.

Charlie They're going to want scapegoats.

John This isn't our fault!

Charlie This is true. It also true that loans were approved on the basis of our reports.

John The board didn't approve those loans on the basis of our reports! You, you, said so yourself. They approved those loans on the basis of tripling the bank's lending within five years and that came from Howard.

Charlie And he'll be quietly retired. It won't stop them coming after us.

Charlie There's a system at stake here. And the way they protect the system is by sentencing the few –

John Sentence?! *Stop.*

Charlie I'm just saying you and me –

John *I said stop.*

Charlie We've got to be smart.

John I am not a criminal. I have done nothing wrong.

Charlie Our reports were on the optimistic side . . .

John Are you wearing a wire?

Charlie What?

John Are you wearing a wire?

Little pause.

Charlie You're serious. You're . . . (*Laughing.*) You're
actually . . .

*John lunges at Charlie, searches for a wire, Charlie
pushes him off.*
John heads for the bathroom.

FIVE

The bathroom.
*John opens a cubicle door. A six-foot seal and penguin
are attempting sex. Upon realising the intrusion they stop
and stare at John. He stares at them; slowly he closes the
door . . .*
Frank appears.

John (*fright*) Jesus!

Frank You got to pull yourself together, sport.

John is beside himself with fear.

We all get the jitters from time to time. I've been a hunted
man.

John Stay away from me.

Frank I know what it's like. You feel them closing in, the
noose tightening.

John urgently chucks water from the sink on his face.

Anybody been staking the house? What about the phone?
You checked the phone?

John No, no –

Frank (*a frantic echo*) What about a wire? Was he wearing a wire?

John STAY AWAY FROM ME, YOU FUCKING SHIT!

Frank (*full of charm*) But we're inseparable, you and me.

John (*to himself*) I'm not listening.

Frank You're going to have to listen sometime.

John *You're not even here!*

Frank Details. You're just as unreal as I am.

John turns away from him and speaks to himself in the mirror.

John I'm not a criminal.

Frank Like father like son.

John I've done no different to anyone else in my position.

Frank My experience, that's not the best defence.

John I don't need a defence!

Frank You're just the guy the world wants to see fail.

John Fuck them.

Frank Guys like you, living high on the hog.

John Whatever I'm paid, it's nothing like what I'm worth!

Frank You'd be looking at ten years . . .

John turns to Frank in terror.

A failure. Everything you've worked for . . .

John is on the floor, holding his knees.

It might not come to that . . .

Maybe you'll just get a fine. A suspension, maybe. Our crimes are the hardest to nab. Most businesses just write

off the loss. Unless . . . unless the losses are so big . . .
unless the losses hit people's savings . . .

John Fuck 'em.

Frank Ordinary Americans and their checking accounts.

John The day I'm sorry is the day I'm dead in the water.

Frank That's the spirit!

John I need to get out of here.

Frank What do you say we hit the town? I know just the
place.

Frank heads for a cubicle.

John What are you doing? Exit's that way.

Frank What's it matter? You accept the larger absurdities,
you accept the small.

Frank disappears inside the cubicle.
*The Penguin emerges from another cubicle, stops,
stares . . .*

Penguin Chivalry is dead.

SIX

Club.
*John dances in wild abandonment. Frank is also
possibly here; a shadowy, old-school, dancing, flickering
presence. The music blares, the lights are erratic . . .*
*The lights giving way to the sight of a woman dancing
alone, swaying slowly, her hair hanging forward over her
face.*

John Grace?

She lifts her head up, dramatically.

Grace Dance with me.

She does an impressive dance move.

John Are you following me?

She dances around him seductively.

Don't think I don't know what you're doing.

Grace's voice has taken on a strange, hypnotic quality.

Grace Just a couple of questions, John.

John You're trying to set me up.

Grace People are going to want answers.

John What people want is someone to blame.

Grace Eighty billion's a lot of money, where did it all go, John?

John Why are you asking me?

Grace Reckless loans were made, made by you.

John Show me one loan the committee didn't sign off on!

Grace Did you misrepresent the nature of those loans?

John No.

Grace If they take a closer look at your reports what do you think they'll find?

John Think this is your big opportunity, your comeback?!

Grace Development projects whose costs overran?

John No.

Grace Developers that got loans for projects that didn't exist?

John No.

Grace Phoney intermediary companies, overpaid US consultants –

John No

Grace That's what Latin America's all about, right?

John No.

Grace Yes.

John No.

Grace You put your bank's future in jeopardy.

John No.

Grace You lent freely until the point of collapse –

John Nooooooooo –

The music grows louder. John goes wild on the dance floor, Grace disappears; the lights go epileptic . . .
 A Figure, dressed in a suit identical to John's, holding a briefcase appears.

Figure The gun is an instrument of both Chaos and Order.

The Figure walks towards John.

Tilt your head.

John obeys, tilts his head to the side; as he does so a liquid sound emits.

Sounds like liquid. Doesn't it?

John breathes, closes his eyes.

Is it a voluntary liquidation?

The Figure hands John his briefcase.

Why don't you hold on to this?

John takes the case.

It'll make you feel better.

He recedes . . .

Promise.

SEVEN

Argentina. An office.
John wipes his forehead. He is clearly on edge, agitated.
The Minister appears, wearing his military uniform.

John Thank you for seeing me at such short notice.

Minister Not at all. Please. What can I do for you?

John I'm afraid there's been a mix-up. At the bank. This is actually embarrassing . . .

Minister (*wafts his hand*) Please . . .

John It's our fault entirely . . . we haven't processed, that is renewed, your credit lines because of a delay. I won't bore you with the details but, but, to get back on track – and it's a formality really – I need you to pay off any outstanding debts you have with us first.

Minister I see.

John At which point we will immediately – and I will personally see to it – get your credit lines up and running again.

Minister No more credit unless my government pays up?

John Like I say, it's a formality, really.

Minister That puts me in a difficult position.

John What's the difficulty?

Minister You're talking about a lot of money . . .

John (*laughs*) This is true.

The Minister smiles.

Minister There appears to be a lot of malfunctioning credit departments right now. You are not the first banker to visit me today, Mr Anderson. I will tell you the same

85

as I told them: this is Argentina, not Mexico . . . in a stampede the herd cannot tell the difference. We will of course pay off any outstanding loans.

John Well that's . . . much appreciated.

Minister It will take some time to arrange.

John Of course. How much time? An idea would be helpful.

Minister I will look into the matter –

John You think you're the first borrower I've visited? You're not. Not even close. And like you, everyone keeps telling me they're not Mexico. *I know that*. The problem is, my boss, he doesn't.

Minister Mexico is a big problem for you. You are their biggest lender, no? It seems to me you have enough problems without creating more.

John You think it's business as usual right now?

Minister I think you should remember your own rule: never kill off your customers. Go back to New York –

John I can't go back.

Minister Your boss will understand.

John You had the money and now, now, now it's time to pay up.

Minister This meeting is over.

John No, no, you are going to pay what you –

Minister I am not asking, Mr Anderson – Time for you to leave.

John You're not listening.

Minister It is time for you to leave

John What did you just say?

Minister *Ya es hora que –*

John I don't speak Spanish.

Minister Who is speaking Spanish?

John I DO NOT SPEAK SPANISH.

Minister *Quien esta hablando Español?*

John I don't understand.

Minister *Salte de aqul, ya!*

John I don't understand.

Minister *Boludo! Estas tonto?*

John I DON'T UNDERSTAND.

He pulls out a gun.

You understand this?

Minister *Hombre, que estas haciendo?*

John What am I doing?

Minister *Calma, calmate.*

John WHAT DOES IT LOOK LIKE I'M DOING?

EIGHT

A light bulb, table, chair; the sound of a ticking clock.
Character 1 and Character 2 are staring at John.

John Who are you?

No response.

Where am I?

Character 1 Somewhere you can cause no harm.

Little pause.

John I want a lawyer.

Character 1 Murder is the logical extension of business. Charlie Chaplin said that.

Character 2 Funny guy.

Character 1 Hilarious.

John I want to make a phone call.

Character 1 John's in business. Aren't you, John?

Character 2 What kind of business?

John I want to make a phone call.

Character 2 Do we look like police to you?

Little pause.

John How long have I been here?

Character 1 Some questions have to be asked.

John What am I doing here?

Character 1 You see that's normally the *first* question people ask.

Character 2 (*impersonates such an incredulous person*) 'What am *I* doing here?'

Character 1 Interestingly, he didn't.

Character 2 Very interesting.

Character 1 It's like he already knew why. That was *very* convincing, by the way.

Character 2 Thank you.

John You tell me why I'm here or let me go!

Character 1 yawns.

Character 1 I couldn't sleep last night.

Character 2 Could you not?

Character 1 My mind was so alive.

Character 2 I slept like I'd been murdered.

Character 1 The same question rattling around and around . . .

Character 2 What was the question?

Character 1 There's a bomb, okay, and it's your job to make it.

Character 2 Am I a physicist?

Character 1 No. You're the man who screws in the bolts, does the welding.

Character 2 And your question is, would I screw in the bolts and do the welding?

Character 1 Very good. I kept thinking about it in bed. Does that man matter?

Character 2 The Cold War keeps you awake at night?

Character 1 I don't worry about the Cold War. I *do* worry about what next.

Character 2 You worry about it *ending*?

Character 1 I worry about what will take its place. Something will.

They stare at each other for a brief moment, then turn their attention to John.

Where was I?

Character 2 Does that man matter?

Character 1 I came to the realisation that he did.

Character 2 He would say he was just doing his job.

Character 1 He may well say that.

Character 2 He would say he just screwed in the bolts.

Character 1 Why don't we ask him?

Both *Do you matter?*

John I . . . I don't understand.

Character 2 produces bound sticks of dynamite, an alarm clock strapped on. He chucks the dynamite at John, who catches it in terror.

Character 1 Four wires across the top. Blue, yellow, green and red obviously. There's always a red. One wire stops the countdown and saves your day. Two wires have no effect whatsoever. The forth detonates and fucks up your day. We'll be outside of the building, of course.

Little pause.

John I don't believe you.

Character 1 What are you finding hard to imagine?

John This isn't real.

Character 1 This is Argentina. In Argentina people disappear.

John You can't do this.

Character 1 Build a bomb and walk away?

Character 2 He did.

Character 1 You did.

John I haven't – there's been a mistake!

Character 2 looks at the time.

Character 1 Running out of time?

John You've got the wrong man!

Boom . . . an explosion resolves into a ringing telephone.
John jolts awake. He answers the ringing phone.

Hello?

Split scene:

Charlie It's me. I'm at the airport.

John Charlie?

Charlie I'm at the airport.

John What time is it?

Charlie You're sleeping?!

John What? No. I'm, I'm –

Charlie You need to wake up right now.

John I thought you were in Brazil till –

Charlie Shut up. I went to their Central Bank today, and looked at their figures.

John They let you do that?

Charlie I didn't give them a *choice*.

John What, what did you . . . ?

Charlie It's going down.

John What'd you . . . ?

Charlie They're going down, we're going down –

John What are you talking about?

Charlie I looked at their figures and . . . there's a giant hole. They're bankrupt.

Little pause.

The whole continent's about to explode.

End of Act Three.

No interval.

Act Four

ONE

The Bank. Men's room.
  Rick and Philip, side by side at the urinal.

Philip I'm telling you, the hotel across the street does a better breakfast.

Rick I don't believe you.

Philip Trust me. It's better.

Rick But it's the same hotel?

Philip Same hotel. Different breakfasts.

Rick Different menus?

Philip Same menus.

  Little pause.

Rick Different recipes?

Philip Identical recipes.

  Little pause.

Rick Ingredients?

Philip It's a chain.

Rick Same ingredients.

Philip Same biscuits. Same gravy. *Different* breakfast.

Rick Huh. That's what you eat for breakfast? Biscuits and gravy?

Philip Sometimes. What?

Rick Nothing. I just didn't have you down as the type.

Philip Type? You judge a person by their breakfast?

Rick It's a revelatory meal.

Philip An important meal. Okay. But revelatory?

Rick Take the Scottish –

Philip Wait. You judge a *nation* by its breakfast?

Rick At their most vulnerable they turn to sheep's guts. I respect that.

Little pause.

Philip What do Froot Loops say about me?

John comes out from the cubicle, washes his hands, and uses the drier.

Rick It doesn't work.

John tries the drier again.

Philip It doesn't work.

John tries it again.

Rick It doesn't work.

John Don't look at me like I'm insane.

Philip The definition of insanity is to keep doing the same thing over and over and over expecting a different outcome.

TWO

The Bank. Conference room.
  Howard, Charlie, John and Holmes. Ties and blazers are off, sleeves rolled; you get the impression they've been here a while. Frank sits in the corner casually throwing screwed-up paper balls into the bin.

93

Charlie We have to lend more. In light of what we now know what alternative –

Holmes More of the same is not an alternative.

Frank (*to John*) You should eat something.

Holmes It's a deferral.

Frank (*to John*) You look like shit.

Charlie It's Armageddon deferred.

Frank (*to John*) When'd you last sleep?

Holmes For how long?

Charlie How long?!

Frank (*to John*) How long can you keep this up?

Charlie We're going down.

Frank You're going down.

Holmes I KNOW THAT.

Charlie This model has worked, it can work again, we just need some time –

Holmes Oh my God, have I really been speaking to myself for twelve hours?!

Charlie Frankly, I think you've been speaking above your pay grade, sweetheart.

Holmes Sweetheart?

Howard What time is it?

Frank (*to John*) Who's that guy?

Holmes We have five more minutes.

Frank (*to John*) The one who keeps looking at you.

Holmes Howard, you have got to take the losses now.

Frank (*to John*) Is that something in his ear?

Holmes Time to tell the board . . . it's over.

Charlie You *cannot* be serious.

Frank (*to John*) There's something in his ear.

Holmes You keep going, you mislead the regulators –

Charlie Fuck the regulators.

Frank (*to John*) Fuck, there's two of them.

Holmes *You're* fucked if you knowingly misrepresent your statements . . .

Frank (*to John*) It's the FBI.

Holmes Never mind misleading investors and stockholders. It could go criminal!

A Staffer enters.

Staffer Mr Richman? They're ready for you upstairs.

Howard nods. Tthe Staffer leaves.

Howard Let me get this straight, I'm about to stand in front of the entire board with my breeches round my ankles giving them the why and wherefores of how we fucked up, how their banks going to be being wiped out because of it, and you're giving me . . . nothing?

No one says anything for a second.

Howard I HAVE TO GIVE THEM SOMETHING.

Charlie Then for Christ's sake, Howard, listen to me!

Holmes Yout IQ sure as hell doesn't rise with your voice.

Charlie We can do this, let's go up there, me and you –

Howard Peddle the same horseshit, you think I can take that in there? No, I'm going up there alone.

95

John You're not alone.

Howard What?

John You're not alone. We're not alone. The problem's not only in this room.

Howard I think I know how fucking big the problem is.

John We are fucked. We are so fucked – all of us.

Charlie Have you just woken up?

Frank laughs.

John Shut up.

Charlie You shut the fuck up.

John But we're not the only bank that's fucked – and that's good, that's very good.

Howard You've ninety seconds to give me something coherent, starting now.

John All of the biggest banks in this country have placed their bets in Latin America, bets so huge, not one of them will survive this. It's not just the banks that are going down, it's the American economy. Our government is not going to let that happen. Mexico needs rescuing. We go to the IMF.

Charlie The *Fund*. Oh that's brilliant.

John They can keep Mexico solvent.

Charlie They have nowhere near that kind of money!

John They don't. Governments do. And I'm not just talking about America.

Howard Fucking Lloyds Bank has got more capital down there than we do.

John Right, there's the British, German, Japanese . . .

Howard So, so, to save their banks they kick in money to the IMF.

John The IMF lends it. Mexico stays solvent.

Howard But only, only, if Mexico agrees to keep up its debt payments to the banks . . .

He turns to Holmes.

Howard Could that fucking work?

Holmes It stretches their credibility as a neutral agency. But it wouldn't exceed their legal authority.

Howard This is good . . . This could be a way out.

Charlie So it is, like I said, we do in fact need to keep giving them money.

Howard No this is much better: it's not our money we're giving . . .
Margie, my wife, likes the Hamptons. Always wants to go to the Hamptons. Me, I don't care for it. I don't like being backed up to the sea. I don't like being backed up to anything. I like options. Exits . . .

He leaves. Charlie and Holmes by the door..

Charlie You want to go for a drink?

Holmes I don't think so.

Charlie Because what? I'm a banker?

Holmes Partly. But mostly because you're a cunt.

He leaves. followed by Charlie.
John and Frank:

Frank You bought yourself some time.

John I just saved our asses.

Frank Questions are still going to be asked –

John sits.

You know I'm right . . .

Frank sits; they are seated back to back, heads touching: a shared cranium.

In jail they tell you when to eat, when to shit, shower, sleep . . . to sleep . . . imagine that. It's a relief. A relief, I tell you. No more laying there awake at night, keeping the hustle going, every day thinking today is the day the jig is up, every knock at the door, it's a nightmare.

John pulls away.

Frank It'd break your mother's heart, of course. For her to have to see you like that, her boy in jail.
You think she'd understand, John? Think she'd come visit? Even after you'd let her down like that? (*Imitates Mother's crying voice.*) After what your father did to us, everything we went through, how we suffered, how could you, John, how could you –

John lunges for Frank, forcing him down on to the desk. He strangles him. Frank's legs kick horribly; John reaches for the heavy ashtray and bludgeons him to death with it. He steps back, deeply shaken. He does not take his eyes off the limp body. The lights flicker. Howard appears.

Howard You're free this evening?

John's hands and shirt are spattered in blood. His gaze is still on Frank.

John Yes . . . (*Turns to Howard.*) I'm free.

Howard You're coming to Park Avenue.

THREE

Park Avenue. Howard's apartment.

Chief executives from major banks and the Treasury. They have glasses of whisky but the atmosphere is far from jovial; it is fraught. All the Bankers (chief executives) are American. John remains blood-splattered.

Treasury You're asking me to throw away tax dollars on foreigners.

Banker 1 The politics will be awful, we understand this –

Treasury You have no idea. Tax dollars for ten years of bankers' mistakes?!

Banker 2 I wouldn't call economic forces beyond our control 'bankers' mistakes'.

Treasury What would you call this clusterfuck?

Banker 1 (*pointedly*) We didn't raise interest rates.

Treasury You leveraged America!

Howard No one's throwing away tax dollars.

Treasury You expect me – never mind Congress – to believe they'll pay us back? Bailing out Mexico sends the wrong message.

Banker 2 Now is not the time for Old Testament righteousness, however good it feels –

Banker 1 Brazil and Argentina are weeks away from insolvency –

Treasury If we bail out Mexico we'll have them all lining up! We can't bail them all out.

Little pause.

You have got to be kidding me . . .

99

Banker 1 There isn't a Latin American country that hasn't borrowed heavily –

Banker 2 They're falling down like flies.

Treasury You're talking about a continent of more than three hundred million people!

Howard Half of them are in Brazil, and it's next –

Banker 1 We have four and a half billion in Brazil.

Banker 2 We've over three billion but our exposure in Venezuela is –

Treasury *America* is in its deepest recession since the thirties. Or did you not notice?

Howard is about to weigh in but is cut dead by the Treasury.

Americans have seen nothing but hard times since nineteen seventy-*three*. *Americans* have been left waiting in gas lines, wondering just where in hell the dream went as the worst inflation in a century decimates their jobs, and the highest interest rates in memory make owning their own home a fantasy. And you're talking about rescuing a continent of foreigners with their tax dollars –

John We're talking about rescuing the Western world's banking system!

The interruption is a surprise. Howard makes to speak but John continues.

Because it's that or a worldwide fucking nightmare. If we go down, we're taking everybody with us. Fourteen hundred banks across America have placed their bets with us, every loan we package involves hundreds of other banks, international and national. So unless you want millions of Americans to lose their savings, their jobs, their healthcare, and any other insurance they have, their homes as foreclosures sweep across the country –

Howard There really is no alternative, is what he's saying.

Banker 1 It's what we're all saying.

Pause.

Treasury Any deal would have to include something in it for us. If this administration's funding the biggest bailout in financial history, it's coming with a price. Starting with us getting their crude for a fire-sale price.

Banker 2 You are one hard-hearted son of a bitch.

Treasury I'm just getting the best deal for the taxpayer.

Banker 1 The priority is avoiding imminent region-wide default, not extracting your pound of flesh –

Banker 2 Any oil deal will be controversial.

Howard We need a deal on the table that's acceptable to Mexico and we need it fast.

Banker 1 The IMF are going to have conditions of their own, market reforms . . .

Banker 2 The IMF needs to be brought in line, there isn't time to fuck around with conditions.

Howard The IMF need to make Mexico an offer they can't refuse.

The Fund/IMF (a woman) appears. Everyone falls silent.

Fund Something you quickly learn at the Fund: no one is ever happy to see you.

FOUR

Howard's apartment. Continuous.
Towards the end of a long night. John and Howard:

John This isn't going to work.

Howard Any bail-out was always going to come with conditions. No one hands out money without strings attached.

John If defaulting appears a more attractive offer than what we put on the table that's exactly what they'll do. Why take that risk? We should go back in there and force the IMF to ease their demands –

Howard The only way you make people do what you want is with leverage: you either have something they need, or something they fear. We are out of leverage.

John So let's lean on the Treasury –

Howard They're having a fucking field day in there. This is their golden opportunity to remake Mexico –

John Then it's not going to happen.

Howard We make it happen. That's what we do. In fifteen years I've seen things you would not believe. Things people said were impossible. When you're prepared to do whatever it takes, everything's possible. And we will do whatever it takes because we don't lose, John. You hear? We do not lose.

You'll be heading out to Mexico with the IMF, most of the debts in your portfolio.

John And Charlie's.

Howard Charlie's taking a step back. You know these loan agreements inside out –

John A step back? What do you mean?

Howard Whilst the investigations under way. You'll be on the first flight –

John Charlie's being investigated?

Howard The board has some questions. He made some reckless bets, he pushed for the expansion of the division. Right?

A very little pause.

John Right.

An almost smile, a tiny confirmation creeps across Howard's lips.

Howard Wall Street's full of sheep that think they're lions. And you were a sheep too, John. But I saw the lion in you, the killer. I saw it because there's a killer in here too . . .

FIVE

Mexico City. Palace balcony.
Minister addressing a huge celebratory crowd.

Minister This financial plague is wreaking greater and greater havoc throughout the world. As in medieval times, it is scourging country after country. It is transmitted by rats and its consequences are unemployment and poverty, industrial bankruptcy and speculative enrichment . . .

The defiant crowd roar and cheer.

SIX

Mexico City. Minister's office.
The Minister slides across a file.

Minister I will not agree to this. I cannot agree to this.

No one says anything.

These proposals are worse than the ones I rejected.

Fund That was twelve days ago. In that time your economy has contracted.

Minister With these proposals our economy will not only contract, it will collapse.

Fund These are much needed structural reforms.

Minister That will condemn the middle classes to poverty, overnight.

Fund Long term the benefits of a liberalised market, a privatisation programme –

Minister You want the minimum wage cut by a third!

Fund A commitment to fiscal austerity is part of the programme.

Minister Fiscal austerity? Thirty per cent of our people earn less than three dollars a day.

John That's not our problem.

The Minister turns, tosses the file.

Minister The people will not accept your conditions.

Fund We will not sign off on a bail-out unless you do.

Minister Bail-out, bail-out; bail-out – can we stop calling it that? The money will not go towards paying off our debt. Towards helping Mexico. (*To John.*) You must give up the idea you can keep on earning interest on our debt.

John You're insolvent. You need to give up the idea you can negotiate.

Fund We will not support a bail-out that asks the banks to accept losses.

Minister Losses! My country will have paid the money we borrowed three times over and still we won't have touched the principle. Meanwhile we are fighting forty per cent unemployment . . .

Fund Tough policies are needed to ensure this does not happen again. The Fund strongly believes that simply saving people from their mistakes only encourages more of the same behaviour.

Minister There is a price to pay for our economic woes. I know this, the people know this, but we have to be realistic. It cannot *only* be Mexicans who pay the bill.

John The American taxpayer appreciates your gratitude.

Minister The banks must pay too! Twenty-seven million dollars a day, eighteen thousand seven hundred and fifty dollars a minute, every single minute, to the banks in interest –

John That's the price of using someone else's money!

Minister Half our population is under the age of fifteen, you are punishing children!

They are unmoved.

Do you really want a failed state on your border with a frontier running from California to Texas? People are already fleeing. They wedge themselves under the box cars of trains and cling on for hundreds of miles. They wade across the Rio Grande. It used to be four hundred a day crossing the border. Now, for the first time ever, it's a thousand. You want to turn that stream into a flood?

John It's nothing compared to the tide of misery coming your way, if you do not pay your debts.

There would be blood on the streets and there would be no relief.

Minister But there would still be a Mexico. The same cannot be said for your banks.

John Let's cut the crap, shall we?

Fund I think we should take five –

John You're building not one, but a five-mansion complex for yourself outside of Mexico City. The money for which comes from government coffers, and that's a drop in the ocean compared to the hundred and sixty-five million you deposited in your own account. You, your wealthy friends, the amount of money, the billions you've taken out this country is staggering . . . Your son is deputy minister, your mistress minister of tourism, your sisters, cousins all hold government positions. You don't care about Mexicans, you care about your own survival, about money and power.

Minister And I cannot survive this!

John What if the people that keep you in power, the wealthy you're dependent upon for political survival, were protected?

Minister Protected?

John From the reforms.

John turns to the Fund.

Fund The IMF's view on the distribution of austerity between various sectors of society is . . . flexible. We understand that at the top of society there are what we identify as modernising elements. These people could be protected as it is the Fund's belief that they benefit everyone. Not just yourself.

The Minister takes the pen and signs.
The jubilant protest sounds resolve into anger and rioting.
A Mexican spectre appears before John.
John leaves . . .

SEVEN

The livid sound of riots and mayhem.

John is walking away from it all – the petrol bombs and raging crowds.

John is confronted by a mob of journalists, all in business suits. They rapidly fire questions at him, microphones in his face . . .

Journalist 1 Will the harsh austerity agreed by Mexico be a template for Latin America?

Journalist 2 Do you believe your fiscal targets are credible in a third-world country?

Journalist 3 Would you agree that this is just the beginning of bail-outs for Mexico?

Journalist 2 Name a country that committed to this kind of austerity and grew?

Journalist 2 Shit shower shave or shave shit shower?

Journalist 3 Does the United states feel a moral obligation to help its Southern neighbours?

Journalist 2 Family man or single?

Journalist 1 Bourbon or scotch?

Journalist 2 How will this bail-out affect the American worker?

Journalist 1 What flavours your milkshake?

Journalist 3 Do you understand what you've done here?

John What we've done here is an historic achievement!

The Journalists become a threatening mass. All now wear day of dead face paint.

Journalist 1 Conquistadors! Murderers! Thieves!

Journalist 2 Mine-owners! Barons! Priests!

Journalist 3 Ranchers! Loggers! Generals!

Journalist 1 Opening our veins!

Journalist 2 Our gold! Our silver!

Journalist 3 Our exploitation! Your plunder!

Journalist 1 Our copper, our tin . . .

Grace appears.
The Day of the Dead Journalists continue their
above lines in a low whispery chant underscoring
Grace's speech.

Grace Their closed hospitals, redundant schools,
dilapidated factories, their unemployed, their dispossessed,
the desperate drama of millions, their bewilderment, their
rage, riots, restructuring, their trashed lives, lost generation,
lost decade, lost GDP, their targets, roads leading to
nowhere, ransacked shelves, inferno cities, waking
nightmares, dying dreams, young men wading through
rivers, young men clinging on to the underside of trains,
the dead in the rivers, the dead on the tracks, a thousand
lonely suicides, borders, blissed-out junkies, cocaine,
cartels, barefoot children, tiny graves, garbage-pickers,
shacks, shanties, squalor, vacant eyes, hunger,
hopelessness, fear, disease, death, misery, death, despair,
death, death, death . . .

Mexican mariachi music explodes forth, a celebratory
sound. A macabre carnival ensues. John is pulled along
into a dancing crowd of Day of the Dead face-painted
figures . . .
A hand is placed on his shoulder from the mass –
it's Howard, and he's wearing a sombrero.

Howard Just the man I've been looking for!

John Howard?

Howard The board couldn't be happier.

John What, what are you . . .?

Howard This country's a cash cow for us, we hope they never repay!

John What are you doing here?

Howard We wanted to show our appreciation. What do you say, *Vice President*? I understand your concerns . . . you think you'll be managing a smaller department. Nothing could be further from the truth, with these rescheduling fees and interest payments our projected profits are expected to rise by *sixty-six* per cent in the next three years. Looks like this crisis will be a true windfall . . .

He vanishes.

John Howard . . .?

A Banker sprays a champagne bottle and roars. Day of the Dead figures are begging; a musician passes playing an accordion.

Figures *Señor, por favor, señor . . .*

John pulls away from them. They grab his clothes; he loses his blazer.

Por favor, por favor . . .

John is pushing people out of the way. Suddenly Charlie grabs hold of him.

Charlie Listen, no hard feelings.

John Charlie?

Charlie You did me a favour.

A Day of the Dead figure pours them both champagne.

The market's so hot right now, even if you've done reasonably well at your job you can move to another bank and double your salary. I told them to triple it.

John But the investigation . . . ?

Charlie Talent can go anywhere right now. And nobody wants an exodus of talent . . .

Charlie vanishes.
  A Pensioner with a Day of the Dead face appears, stares at John . . .

Pensioner I have no other way.

The Pensioner walks towards John.

I have no other way.

The Pensioner suddenly slits his own throat; his blood spatters John. John backs away and into another figure who hangs herself, and then into another who overdoses, and another who jumps to their death.
  He screams. The music scratches and cuts.
  Black.
  He is on the floor, alone, covered in his own sweat.

John I need to get out of here.

Frank in prison gear is mopping the blood off the floor.

Frank There's no way out, kid.

Frank is much older, shuffling, wheezing.

John Frank?

Frank Careful, will yer? I just mopped that.

John Frank . . . I'm . . . (*On the verge of tears.*) I'm so glad to see you.

Frank continues mopping, whistles faintly.

You're not glad to see me?

Frank looks vacantly at John.

It's me . . . John.

Frank No John ever came to see me.

John I'm here now.

Frank Nobody ever came see me. All these years . . .

He hacks up some phlegm into a tissue.

Emphysema. I suppose I earned it. Quit while you can, whoever listened to that? (*He lights a cigarette.*) Not me. Not ever. Quit while you can . . . while you're ahead . . . but the con is a beautiful thing; a beautiful thing to be inside. And there was none more beautiful than the last. I took my time reeling him in, nice and easy. He was mine, hook, line and sinker. The next day, I don't know why, but I drove out to see him. I sat outside his house in my car and saw him crying. And I felt sorry. For him. For his wife. Kids . . .

The day you feel sorry is the day you're dead in the water . . .

He hacks his phlegm again.

Two weeks later I was in here.

He picks up his mop and bucket.

John Don't leave. Don't leave me, don't – *Where are you going?*

Frank Nowhere . . .

He disappears into the dark.

(*Voice only.*) A place where there's no one but yourself with no self left.

John is alone surrounded by darkness. He shoots himself in the head.

EPILOGUE

The Bank. Elevator. Rick and Philip: same guys, different suits. Broadsheets tucked under arm.

Rick The security guard's had a haircut.

Philip I saw that. It's an ambitious haircut.

Rick Didn't we once have that haircut?

Philip It all comes back.

Little pause.

Ask me about the traffic in Athens.

Rick How's the traffic in Athens?

Philip Impressive. The traffic's impressive.

Rick And the heat?

Philip Fatal. Heat's fatal.

Little pause.

Rick Any good dirty words?

Philip *Fantastic* dirty words. *Malackas.*

Rick *Malackas?*

Philip Masturbator. It's a term of affection.

Rick Huh. Who knew?

Little pause.

What are we doing there?

Philip In Greece?

The elevator doors open . . .

We're giving them some money.

Black.

It begins.